DAN MURPHY'S

Classification of Australian Wines

SUN BOOKS · MELBOURNE

Sun Books Pty Ltd, South Melbourne, Victoria 3205, Australia

First published by Sun Books 1974
Copyright © D. F. Murphy, 1974
Maps and graphics © D. F. Murphy, 1974

National Library of Australia
cataloguing in publication data

Murphy, Dan F.
  Dan Murphy's classification of Australian
  wines.–Melbourne: Sun Books, 1974.
  Index.
  ISBN 0 7251 0195 4.

  1. Wine and wine making–Australia.
  I. Title.

  641.220994

Set in Monophoto Times by Modgraphic, Adelaide
Printed in Australia at
The Griffin Press, Adelaide

Table of Contents

DARWIN

ARNHEM

CAPE LONDONDERRY

KIMBERLEY

INDIAN OCEAN

NORTHERN

NORTH EAST
CAPE

GIBSON DESERT

WESTERN AUSTRALIA

GREAT VICTORIA DESERT

SOUTH

Swan
Valley

PERTH
FREMANTLE   Kenwick

GREAT AUSTRALIAN BIGHT

CAPE
NATURALISTE   MARGARET RIVER
CAPE LEEUWIN   Mt. Barker

THE VINEYARD AREAS
OF AUSTRALIA

VINEYARD AREAS

SCALE
100   0   100   200   300   400   500
MILES

The Wine Areas

STATE – South Australia

REGIONS   AREAS

1. Clare – Watervale   (i) Clare
                              (ii) Watervale

2. Barossa Valley and   (i) Barossa Valley
   surrounding Areas   (ii) Barossa Ranges
                              (iii) Adelaide Environs

3. Southern Vales   (i) Reynella/Happy Valley/
                                   Coromandel Valley
                              (ii) McLaren Vale
                              (iii) Langhorne Creek

4. South-east South   (i) Coonawarra
   Australia   (ii) Keppoch

5. Murray Valley   (i) Northern Murray River
                              (ii) Southern Murray River

STATE – Victoria

1. South-west Victoria   (i) Great Western
                              (ii) Avoca
                              (iii) Drumborg

2. Goulburn Valley   (i) Central
                              (ii) Northern

2   Classification of Australian Wines

REGIONS	AREAS
3. North-east Victoria	(i) Corowa/Rutherglen
	(ii) King Valley
	(iii) Taminick
4. Murray Valley	(i) Murray Valley East
	(ii) Murray Valley West
5. Central Victoria	Marong
	Lilydale
6. Yarra Valley	Melbourne Environs
7. Geelong	Waurn Ponds

STATE – New South Wales

1. Hunter Valley and surrounding Areas	(i) Pokolbin/Rothbury
	(ii) Wybong/Sandy Hollow
	(iii) Hunter Flats
	(iv) Mudgee
2. Riverina	(i) Murrumbidgee Irrigation Area
	(ii) Hay
3. Smaller Regions	(i) Forbes
	(ii) Rooty Hill

STATE – Western Australia

1. Swan Valley	(i) Upper Swan
	(ii) Lower Swan

REGIONS	AREAS
2. Busselton/Frankland	(i) Margaret River
	(ii) Mt Barker
3. Yanchep	Gin-Gin

STATE – Queensland

1. South-east Queensland	(i) Roma
	(ii) Southern Highlands

STATE – Tasmania

1. Tasmanian Valleys	(i) Tamar Valley
	(ii) Derwent Valley

How to use Classification Tables

(1) Classification according to vineyards
(2) Classification according to winemaker and label
(3) Classification according to Vintage Year.

Since a very great area for vineyards does not always have very great makers, and since even average quality vineyards can, with a good winemaker, on occasion produce very great wines and since, in addition, not every year is a good year, the three tables have to be used in conjunction.

Say, for example, you wished to know whether Lindeman's Bin 3703 Hunter River Ben Ean Burgundy of 1968 vintage was a great wine. You would look up, first of all, the Classification of Australian Wines according to Maker and Label. There you would find that the Lindeman 4 number label Hunter Valley Burgundy was classified as a 'very great' wine, i.e. it would be very great in a very great year but would not necessarily be so every year it appeared, though Lindeman's might wish to market it only in very great years.

Next you would look up the Classification of Australian Vineyards and you would find that Ben Ean was classified as an 'outstanding' vineyard.

Finally, you would check on the Vintage Chart. Here you would find that 1968 received two stars in the Hunter Valley, which means that it was a good year.

You would know, then, that this particular wine was a great wine but not outstanding.

Classification of Wines and Vineyards

GRADINGS

Description	*Grading*
Top quality	Outstanding
Almost but not quite top quality	Very great
Extremely high quality	Great
High quality	Very good
Worth drinking on special occasions and holding for some time	Good
Bottling Standard but should not be kept long	Standard
Bulk wine – Pleasant every day drinking but not worth keeping	Quaffing

Note: Classification given of vineyards and wines extends only from 'Very good' to 'Outstanding'.

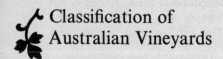# Classification of
Australian Vineyards

RED WINES
OUTSTANDING VINEYARDS

AREA	VINEYARD
Clare	Selected vineyards
Coonawarra	Brand's Laira
	Coonawarra Grape Growers
	Franze
	Grigg
	Hill
	House of Reynell
	Limestone Ridge
	Messenger
	Mildara
	Penfold
	Redbank
	Rouge Homme
	Skinner
	Terra Rossa Wines
	Wynn
Great Western	Concongella
	Great Western
Pokolbin/Rothbury	Ashmans
	Belbourie
	Bellevue
	Ben Ean

RED WINES
OUTSTANDING VINEYARDS (contd.)

AREA	VINEYARD
Pokolbin/Rothbury	Happy Valley
	Herlstone
	Homestead Hill
	Hundred Acre
	Hungerford Hill
	Ivanhoe
	Lake's Folly
	Mt Pleasant
	Oakvale
	Rosehill
	Rothbury Estate
	Tallawanta
	* Bimbadgen
	* Broken Back Estate
	* De Beyers
	* Drayton (Barry)
	* Glen Oak
	* Hermitage
	* Kemp
	* McPherson
	* Mistletoe
	* Oakdale
	* Somerset
	* Tamburlaine
	* The Wilderness
	* Weinkeller Estate
Wybong/Sandy Hollow	Penfold's Wybong Park
	* Chateau Douglas
	* Hollydene

*Vineyards which have not produced sufficient wines for quality to be assessed, but which are in locations which indicate great quality.

8   Classification of Australian Wines

RED WINES
OUTSTANDING VINEYARDS (contd.)

Area	Vineyard
	* Hordern's Wybong Estate
	* Mt Dangar
	* Peachey
	* Richmond Grove
	* Stair
	* Yore
Geelong	* Waurn Ponds
Yarra Valley	* Cester – Coldstream
	* De Pury – Yering
	* Egan – Wantirna South
	* Fergusson – Yarra Glen
Drumborg	* Seppelt

RED WINES
VERY GREAT VINEYARDS

Area	Vineyard
Barossa Valley	Kalimna
	Orlando
	Selected vineyards
Clare	Selected vineyards
Watervale	Selected vineyards
Reynella/Happy Valley/ Coromandel Valley	Happy Valley
	Light
	Marienberg
	Reynella
	Trennert

RED WINES
VERY GREAT VINEYARDS (contd.)

AREA	VINEYARD
	Selected vineyards
McLaren Vale	Amery
	Coriole
	Seaview
Adelaide Environs	Auldana/Magill
Keppoch	Hardy
	Seppelt
	Glenloth
	Lindeman
Avoca	Barry
	Chateau Remy
	Taltarni
Marong	Balgowni
Mudgee	Augustine
	Craigmoor's Eurunderee
	Huntingdon Estate
	Mudgee Wines
	Independent vineyards
Hunter Flats	Fordwich – Elliott
	Tulloch
	Saxonvale
	Branxton – Wyndham Estate
	* Arrowfield
	* Black Hill
	* Bilboa
	* Cecchini
	* Gelstone

*Vineyards which have not produced sufficient wines for quality to be assessed, but which are in locations which indicate great quality.

RED WINES
VERY GREAT VINEYARDS (contd.)

AREA	VINEYARD
	* Glendon Brook
	* Horseshoe
	* Mindaribba
	* Quintella
	* Rosemount
	* Roxburgh
	* Verona
Margaret River	* Selected vineyards
	Pearse
	Westfield
Mt Barker	* Selected vineyards
	Sandalford
	Cullity
	Pannell

RED WINES
GREAT VINEYARDS

AREA	VINEYARD
Barossa Valley	Basedow
	Bernkastel
	Glenview
	Karrawirra
	Liebich
	St Hallett's
	Saltram
	Seppelt

*Vineyards which have not produced sufficient wines for quality to be assessed, but which are in locations which indicate great quality.

RED WINES
GREAT VINEYARDS (contd.)

AREA	VINEYARD
	Wilsford
	Yaldara
	Yalumba
McLaren Vale	D'Arenberg
	Dennis
	Richard Hamilton
	Hardy's Vineyards
	McLaren Park
	Pirramimma
	Ryecroft
	Sigston
	Starr
	Valle d'Oro
	Wirra Wirra
Barossa Ranges	Selected independent vineyards
Langhorne Creek	Metala
	Selected independent vineyards
Corowa/Rutherglen	All Saints (Wahgunyah)
	Balldale (Corowa)
	Calliope (Rutherglen)
	Gayfer (Chiltern)
	Gehrig (Barnawartha)
	Lindeman (Corowa)
	Mia Mia (Rutherglen)
	Rosewood (Rutherglen)
	Seppelt (Rutherglen)
	Stanton & Killeen (Rutherglen)

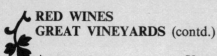

RED WINES
GREAT VINEYARDS (contd.)

AREA	VINEYARD
King Valley	Milawa (Brown)
Taminick	Bundarra (Bailey) Taminick (Booth) Watson
Central Goulburn Valley	Chateau Tahbilk Fitzpatrick (Greytown, Seymour) Osicka (Greytown) Mitchelton
Northern Goulburn Valley	Conte (Ardmona) Curcio (Ardmona) Darveniza (Mooroopna) Gravina (Shepparton) Srimizzi (Ardmona)

WHITE WINES
OUTSTANDING VINEYARDS

AREA	VINEYARD
Geelong	* Waurn Ponds
Yarra Valley	* Cester – Coldstream * De Pury – Yering * Egan – Wantirna South * Fergusson – Yarra Glen
Drumborg	* Seppelt

*Vineyards which have not produced sufficient wines for quality to be assessed, but which are in locations which indicate great quality.

WHITE WINES
OUTSTANDING VINEYARDS (contd.)

AREA	VINEYARD
Barossa Valley	Orlando
Barossa Ranges	Pewsey Vale
	Steingarten
	All vineyards in Eden Valley and Springton
Clare	Selected vineyards
Great Western	Concongella
	Great Western
Wybong/Sandy Hollow	Penfold's Wybong Park
	Hollydene
	* Chateau Douglas
	* Hordern's Wybong Estate
	* Mt Dangar
	* Mount Fern
	* Peachey
	* Richmond Grove
	* Stair
	* Yore
Pokolbin/Rothbury	Ashmans
	Bellevue
	Coolalta
	Glen Elgin
	Herlstone
	Homestead Hill
	Oakdale
	Rothbury Estate
	Stephen
	Sunshine

---

*Vineyards which have not produced sufficient wines for quality to be assessed, but which are in locations which indicate great quality.

WHITE WINES
OUTSTANDING VINEYARDS (contd.)

AREA	VINEYARD
	Tallawanta
	* Bimbadgen
	* Broken Back Estate
	* De Beyers
	* Drayton (Barry)
	* Glen Oak
	* Hermitage
	* Kemp
	* McPherson
	* Mistletoe
	* Oakdale
	* Somerset
	* Tamburlaine
	* The Wilderness
	* Weinkeller Estate

WHITE WINES
VERY GREAT VINEYARDS

AREA	VINEYARD
Barossa Valley	Selected independent vineyards
Barossa Ranges	Selected independent vineyards
Watervale	Quelltaler
	Independent vineyards
Reynella/Happy Valley/ Coromandel Valley	Happy Valley
	Independent vineyards
	Light

---

*Vineyards which have not produced sufficient wines for quality to be assessed, but which are in locations which indicate great quality.

WHITE WINES
VERY GREAT VINEYARDS (contd.)

AREA	VINEYARD
	Marienberg
	Reynella
McLaren Vale	Amery
	Seaview
	Richard Hamilton
Coonawarra	Mildara
	Wynn
King Valley	Milawa (Brown)
Mudgee	Augustine
	Craigmoor
	Independent vineyards
Hunter Flats	Fordwich – Elliott
	Tulloch
	Saxonvale
	Branxton – Wyndham Estate
	* Arrowfield
	* Black Hill
	* Bilboa
	* Cecchini
	* Gelstone
	* Glendon Brook
	* Horseshoe
	* Mindaribba
	* Quintella
	* Rosemount
	* Roxburgh
	* Verona

*Vineyards which have not produced sufficient wines for quality to be assessed, but which are in locations which indicate great quality.

WHITE WINES
GREAT VINEYARDS

AREA	VINEYARD
Barossa Valley	Bernkastel
	Glenview
	Seppelt
	Selected independent vineyards
McLaren Vale	D'Arenberg
	Hardy
Corowa/Rutherglen	All Saints (Wahgunyah)
	Lindeman (Corowa)
Central Goulburn Valley	Chateau Tahbilk
	* Mitchelton
Adelaide Environs	Ewell
	Hope Valley
	Modbury Estate

RED WINES AND WHITE WINES
VERY GOOD VINEYARDS

AREA	VINEYARD
Riverina	Mostly independent growers
	McWilliam
	Wynn
South Australian Murray Valley	Angoves at Renmark and Lyrup
	Gramps at Qualco
	Hamilton at Nildottie
	Hardy at Waikerie
	Seppelt at Qualco

---

*Vineyards which have not produced sufficient wines for quality to be assessed, but which are in locations which indicate great quality.

RED WINES AND WHITE WINES
VERY GOOD VINEYARDS (contd.)

AREA	VINEYARD
	Douglas A. Tolley at Qualco
	TST at Waikerie
	Yalumba at Waikerie
	Mostly independent growers
Victorian Murray Valley	Best at Lake Boga
	Brown at Mystic Park
	Buller at Beverford
	Mildara at Irymple
	Mostly independent growers
	Seppelt at Barooga
Swan Valley	Adriatic
	Baskerville
	Contreville
	Glenalwyn
	Houghton
	Luisini
	Noack
	Olive Farm
	Parri
	Revelry
	Riverside
	Sandalford
	Sveti Maria
	Twin Hills
	Valencia
	Visnica
	Waldeck
	Westfield
	and many independent growers.

**Explanation of Classification
according to Maker and Label**

Vineyards do not change. Makers do. A classification according to vineyards is valid for many years. A classification according to makers is valid only from year to year.

It would be completely misleading if I classified only vineyards. Vineyard 'A' in an oustanding area might have a very poor winery associated with it and an incompetent maker. If the vineyard classification was followed you would gain the impression that Vineyard 'A' in a good year produced outstanding wines. It would be wrong to give you this incorrect guide.

Therefore, I have also classified wines according to makers (wineries) and the labels attached to their bottles. Most Australian wineries have several grades of wine of the same style. It is necessary to know the grade when I classify a wine from a certain maker as 'very great' or 'great'.

The vineyard classification is based on the assumption that the soil will not change materially for decades. No doubt it will change eventually.

Inside a small area of vineyards one might imagine that, if one were classified as outstanding, all of them should be so classified. This is not the case.

Aspect is a very important factor. Generally, I would be inclined to classify all the vineyards in the Pokolbin hills as 'outstanding' but I would not be prepared to give this grading to Rothbury across the road.

Why?

First, it seems to me that the history of Pokolbin is such that the great red wines have come from the volcanic knobs around Pokolbin. When you leave these mounds of residual basaltic soil, the quality of the reds is downgraded.

Secondly, white wines seem to hold their quality on the clay loams and sandy creek beds of Rothbury and so we have a different classification of vineyards in the Pokolbin/ Rothbury areas according to white and red wines.

However, it is pretty evident that a winery is likely to produce better or worse wines with change of management. Beware then, of a classification of wines and labels.

I envisage that a classifying authority will eventually be set up to re-classify wines every five years or so according to the record of makers over the preceding five years. This means that a classification of wines according to makers and labels should be dated. The one I have given you in this book is marked '1974'. I cannot be held responsible for its accuracy in any year but that.

It may be useful as a guide but its usefulness cannot last beyond six years or so.

In order to understand the reason for my classifying the wines as I have, it is necessary to understand the difficulties besetting those who attempt a classification.

In the present situation, one must link up vineyards with the makers. It would be simple to say that every vineyard in the Pokolbin/Rothbury area was outstanding. In truth, this may well be the case; but to describe each one as such in the existing circumstances would be misleading.

A great deal of emphasis must be laid on the reputation of the wine by the label under which it is sold.

No one can question the position of Lindeman's Straight Ben Ean reds sold under the four number label. They are, purely and simply, very great wines and have been so for very many years.

Similarly the impact which Max Lake's wines have had on the Australian wine world, even in spite of the shortness of time that he has spent making wine, places his reds in the 'very great' category.

It could be that Jim Robert's 'Belbourie' vineyard will one day be producing wines which will be proclaimed universally as 'outstanding'. The vineyard is possibly one of the greatest in Australia. We do not know, and we cannot give it prominence until it has earned the right to be ranked as one of the top in Australia.

Similar reasoning follows all through the classification. A vineyard in a 'great' area might not be classified as 'great' because it has not had a long enough history of producing great wines. Perhaps it has been exhibiting in shows and has not won many awards. This would weigh against it. Perhaps it has won quite a number of awards but the award winning wines have not been seen by our top wine men outside the shows. This does not give it the right to be called a 'great' vineyard. Perhaps no wines of note at all have been seen from this vineyard but with a change of owner they could begin to appear.

The maker and the vineyard, therefore, are inextricably tied in Australia.

Again many vineyards are simply places where grapes are grown. The proprietor sends his grapes to a winery. Quite often the winery makes a superb wine out of these grapes and wins an award and high praise all over Australia. The vineyard should be classified accordingly, but except in extremely rare cases the label gives no indication as to what particular vineyard produced the grapes. I have no option then but to place these anonymous vineyards in the category simply as 'selected independent vineyards'.

When the Australian wine industry matures sufficiently to realize the importance of these matters we will be able to have a simple categorization of vineyards on their particular worth.

It is the vineyard that matters. Without quality grapes a winemaker cannot produce quality wine. He can simulate it by means of acid and oak flavour and good balance of the ingredients he has to work with but the essential thing, flavour, can come only from the grapes. Top quality wine is obtained only from top quality vineyards.

While I am quite prepared to admit that McWilliam's and a few other makers can produce wines from Riverina vineyards which win gold medals and earn a great deal of laudatory comments from wine experts, these facts alone do not make them great wines. I am using my own experience over very many years to decide that wines from the Riverina do not equal in quality wines from areas I have listed as 'great', 'very great' or 'outstanding'.

As Veronelli, the great wine authority says, you have to take a great number of samples from the area to decide on its overall quality. A few random examples do not constitute a true test. The same reasoning applies to the wines from the Murray Valley areas and the Swan Valley.

Apart from tasting these wines, and tasting is the only criterion which should be used, the possibility of these regions producing the grapes for top quality wines is remote. Long hot summers and flat, slopeless areas make for the very conditions which create flavourless wines.

The ideal way to classify a country's wines would be to take samples from every area over a period of twenty years and submit them to a large tasting panel of wine experts. They should be asked to place the wines in different categories related to the great and not so great wines of the world.

Not knowing where the wines came from, nor under what conditions of growing the grapes ripened, nor who made the wines or how they were made, the results should be fair, unbiased and accurate.

I have endeavoured to approach the problem this way. Every comment I have heard about a wine by an expert has been used by me to mark it up or down accordingly. I have tried to gather in a private tasting room of my imagination all the opinions of wine experts, including my own, on Australian wines over the last thirty years and to categorize the wines accordingly.

When I describe wineries and makers I have endeavoured to give them the name by which they are best known rather than what is legally correct.

e.g. *Yalumba*   *Not S. Smith & Co. Pty Ltd*
      Kaiser Stuhl *Not Barossa Valley Co-operative Pty Ltd*
      Wolf Blass   *Not Bilyara.*

Classification of Australian Wines 1974

According to Maker and Label

RED WINES
OUTSTANDING WINES

AREA	MAKER	LABEL
South Australia	Penfolds Wines	Grange Hermitage
South Australia	Penfolds Wines	St Henri Claret
Clare	Stanley Wine Co.	Leasingham Bin 49 Cabernet
Coonawarra	Redman (O. & L.)	Redman Claret
Coonawarra	Lindeman	Lindeman's Rouge Homme Claret Rouge Homme Cabernet Sauvignon
Coonawarra	Mildara Wines	Mildara Coonawarra: Cabernet Sauvignon Cabernet Shiraz Cabernet Shiraz Malbec
Coonawarra	Penfolds Wines	Penfold's Bin 128 Coonawarra Claret
Coonawarra	Brand (E)	Brand's Laira: Cabernet Sauvignon Cabernet Shiraz
Coonawarra	Wynn	Coonawarra Estate: Cabernet Sauvignon Cabernet Hermitage Hermitage

Area	Maker	Label
Great Western	Seppelts Wines (Great Western)	'Great Western' Special Bin Labels (denoting style of wine, grape composition and year)

RED WINES
VERY GREAT WINES

Area	Maker	Label
South Australian Vineyards	Penfold	Special bin number labels, e.g. Bin 28 Kalimna Shiraz Bin 707 Kalimna Cabernet Sauvignon Bin 389 Cabernet Shiraz Bin 2 Shiraz Mataro Bin 426 Shiraz Oelliade Bin 747 Shiraz
Clare	Birks	Seabrook's 'Birks Dry Red'
Clare	Stanley Wine Co.	Leasingham Bin 43 Burgundy Stanley Shiraz
Clare	St. Clare (J. Barry)	Malbec Shiraz Cabernet Sauvignon Cabernet Malbec Shiraz Cabernet Shiraz

24   Classification of Australian Wines

Area	Maker	Label
South Australian Vineyards	Kaiser Stuhl	Private Bin label giving details of where grapes were grown and sometimes name of grower e.g. Red Ribbon Shiraz 1967 Bin T65 from vineyard of A. E. Materne, Greenock and Special Reserve Bin label
Reynella/ Happy Valley	House of Reynell	Reynella Cabernet Sauvignon
McLaren Vale	Hardy, Thomas	Cabernet Sauvignon
McLaren Vale	Seaview	Cabernet Sauvignon Cabernet Shiraz
McLaren Vale	Coriole (H. Lloyd)	Claret Hermitage
McLaren Vale	Kay Bros.	Amery 'Cabernet Shiraz'
Langhorne Creek	Stonyfell	Metala Claret
Barossa Valley	Saltram	Mamre Brook Cabernet
South Australian Vineyards	Bilyara (Wolf Blass)	Bilyara 'Dry Red Gold Medal' with information as to where the grapes were grown e.g. 'Langhorne Creek' 'Wilton'
Keppoch	Hardy, Thomas	Keppoch 'Cabernet Sauvignon' 'Hermitage' 'Malbec'

Area	Maker	Label
Keppoch	Seppelts Wines	Under Seppelt label plus code number plus grape variety and 'Keppoch' e.g. 'Hermitage 1968/GW176 Keppoch'
Central Goulburn Valley	Tahbilk Pty Ltd	Special Bin Cabernet Sauvignon
Avoca	Chateau Remy	Cabernet Sauvignon, Cabernet/Hermitage
Bendigo	S. Anderson (Marong)	Balgownie: Cabernet Sauvignon Hermitage
Mudgee	Craigmoor	Cabernet Sauvignon Cabernet Shiraz Mudgee Shiraz
Pokolbin/ Rothbury	Elliott	Oakvale Dry Red Tallawanta Hermitage
Pokolbin/ Rothbury	Lindeman	Lindeman's 'Hunter Valley Burgundy' Plus identifying four numbers
Pokolbin/ Rothbury	Max Lake	Cabernet Sauvignon Hermitage
Pokolbin/ Rothbury	McWilliam	Pinot Hermitage Robert Hermitage
Pokolbin/ Rothbury	Rothbury Estate	Rothbury Estate Followed by identifying numbers of blocks e.g. Rothbury Blocks A, B, & E, 1972

AREA	MAKER	LABEL
Pokolbin/ Rothbury	Tulloch	Private Bin Pokolbin Dry Red
Pokolbin/ Rothbury	Tyrrell	Hunter Valley Dry Red, Winemaker's Selection
Blend: McLaren Vale/ Coonawarra	Hardy, Thomas	Reserve Bin: Cabernet Sauvignon
Blend: Barossa Valley/ Barossa Ranges	TST	Private Bin (Bin Numbers) Shiraz-Cabernet.
Wybong/ Sandy Hollow	Penfolds	Wybong Park: Cabernet Sauvignon Hermitage Other grape varieties

RED WINES
GREAT WINES

AREA	MAKER	LABEL
Watervale	Lindeman	Watervale Shiraz Cabernet
Barossa Valley	Basedow	Special Bin Dry Red
Barossa Valley	Orlando	Orlando 'Barossa Hermitage', 'Barossa Cabernet'
Barossa Valley	Kies	Karrawirra: 'Cabernet Sauvignon' 'Cabernet Gros Shiraz'

Area	Maker	Label
South Australian Vineyards	Leo Buring Pty Ltd	Reserve Bin Label e.g. Cabernet Shiraz 1968 The labels give information where the grapes were grown
South Australian Vineyards	Lindeman	Two number label which gives information where the grapes were grown e.g. Bin 50 Burgundy
Barossa Valley	Bernkastel	Langmeil Claret
Barossa Valley	Buring	Black Label Bin 13 Burgundy, Black Label Bin 7 Claret
Barossa Valley	Glenview	Krondorf Claret
Barossa Valley	Kaiser Stuhl	Vintage Cabernet Sauvignon, Vintage Cabernet Shiraz
Barossa Valley/ Angle Vale	Norman	Angle Vale Claret
Barossa Valley	Saltram	Selected Vintage Claret
Barossa Valley	Seppelt	EC4 Hermitage-Cabernet
Barossa Valley	Yalumba	Galway Claret
Barossa Ranges	Buring	Special Bin Label: Eden Valley/Clare Shiraz

AREA	MAKER	LABEL
Barossa Ranges	Hamilton	Springton Hermitage, Springton Claret, Eden Valley Hermitage
Adelaide Environs	Douglas A. Tolley	Pedare: Cabernet Sauvignon Cabernet Shiraz
Reynella/ Happy Valley/ Coromandel Valley	House of Reynell	Reynella Vintage Reserve: Claret Burgundy
Reynella/ Happy Valley/ Coromandel Valley	Light Wines	Light Claret
Reynella/ Happy Valley/ Coromandel Valley	Marienberg	Claret Hermitage
McLaren Vale	Hamilton	McLaren Vale Cabernet Sauvignon
McLaren Vale	Hardy, Thomas	Nottage Hill Claret
McLaren Vale	Kay	Amery: Dry Red Shiraz
McLaren Vale	Southern Vales Co-op.	Special Bin: Cabernet Hermitage
McLaren Vale	Ryecroft	Cabernet Sauvignon
McLaren Vale	Valle d'Oro	Roxton Estate Brookhill Claret Hillcrest Burgundy

AREA	MAKER	LABEL
Langhorne Creek	Bleasdale	Cabernet-Shiraz
Langhorne Creek	Hamilton	Langhorne Creek Hermitage
Langhorne Creek	Lindeman	Langhorne Creek Oeillade Shiraz
Great Western	Best	No. O Claret with neck label showing grape variety and year
Rutherglen/ Corowa	All Saints	Cabernet-Shiraz, Lyre Bird Claret
Rutherglen/ Corowa	Chambers	Seabrook Bottlings of Blue Imperial Blends
Rutherglen/ Corowa	Morris	Cabernet-Shiraz
King Valley	Brown	Milawa: Shiraz-Mondeuse, Cabernet, Cabernet-Shiraz
Taminick	Bailey	Bundarra Hermitage
Taminick	Booth	Taminick Dry Red
Goulburn Valley	Tahbilk Pty Ltd	Chateau Tahbilk Cabernet
Pokolbin/ Rothbury	Belbourie	Belbourie Dry Red
Pokolbin/ Rothbury	Drayton	Bellevue Hermitage
Pokolbin/ Rothbury	House of Reynell	Hungerford Hill Collection: Pokolbin Dry Reds

30 Classification of Australian Wines

AREA	MAKER	LABEL
Pokolbin/ Rothbury	McWilliam	Philip Hermitage
Pokolbin/ Rothbury	Pokolbin Winemakers	Hermitage
Mudgee	Craigmoor	Cabernet Shiraz
Riverina	Calamia	Bin 17 Troia
Riverina	McWilliam	Private Bin: Cabernet Sauvignon, Cabernet-Shiraz

BLENDS	MAKER	LABEL
Hunter/ McLaren Vale	Hardy, Thomas	Reserve Bin Burgundy
McLaren Vale/ Barossa Valley/ Coonawarra/ Hunter	Hardy, Thomas	Reserve Bin Claret
Hunter/Clare/ Coonawarra	Lindeman	Auburn Burgundy Nyrang Claret
Hunter/ McLaren Vale/ Coonawarra	Mildara	Reserve Bin Cabernet Shiraz
Wybong/ South Australia	Penfold	Special Bin Label: Bin 333
Langhorne Ck./ Barossa Valley	Stonyfell	Vintage Claret
Barossa Valley/ Barossa Ranges	Stonyfell	Private Bin Claret
Barossa Valley/ Murray Valley	TST	Tollana: Claret Burgundy

RED WINES
VERY GOOD WINES

AREA	MAKER	LABEL
Clare	Sevenhill	Dry Red Table Wine
Barossa	Basedow	Special Bin Dry Red
Barossa	Buring	Chateau Leonay: Vintage Hermitage Vintage Burgundy
Barossa	Chateau Rosevale	Vintage Claret Vintage Burgundy
Barossa	Chateau Yaldara	Claret Burgundy
Barossa	Chatterton	Cabernet Shiraz
Barossa	Glen View	Burgundy Claret
Barossa Valley	Kaiser Stuhl	Bin 33 Claret
Barossa	Karlsberg	Cabernet-Sauvignon
Barossa	Orlando	Miamba Vintage Hermitage Cabernet
Barossa	Rovalley	Cabernet Shiraz Shiraz Claret
Barossa	St Hallett's	Carl Special Dry Red Claret
Barossa Ranges	Henschke	Mt Edelstone Claret Hermitage Hill of Grace
Clare	Stanley Wine Co.	Clare Special Claret
Adelaide Environs	Douglas A. Tolley	Pedare: Claret Red Hermitage

32 Classification of Australian Wines

Area	Maker	Label
Adelaide Environs	Wynn	Modbury Estate Claret Huntersfield Burgundy Huntersfield Claret
Reynella/ Happy Valley/ Coromandel Valley	Happy Valley	Cabernet Sauvignon Hermitage
Reynella/ Happy Valley/ Coromandel Valley	House of Reynell	Reynella Bin 2 Dry Red
Reynella/ Happy Valley	Paul Trennert	Cabernet Sauvignon Hermitage
McLaren Vale	D'Arenberg	Cabernet Sauvignon Cabernet Shiraz Burgundy
McLaren Vale	Dover Wine Co.	Claret
McLaren Vale	Hardy, Thomas	McLaren Vale Estate Hermitage
McLaren Vale	Johnston	Pirramimma: Shiraz, Cabernet Shiraz
McLaren Vale	Merrivale	Cabernet Shiraz Shiraz
McLaren Vale	Ryecroft	Shiraz
McLaren Vale	South Coast Winery (K. Genders)	McLaren Park Shiraz
Langhorne Creek	Bleasdale	Bremer Claret Shiraz
Northern S.A. Murray Valley	Berri Co-op.	Mine Host: Cabernet Sauvignon Cabernet Shiraz

AREA	MAKER	LABEL
Southern S.A. Murray Valley	Hamilton	Nildottie Hermitage
Northern S.A. Murray Valley	Renmano	Montessa: Claret Cabernet Malbec
Northern S.A. Murray Valley	Toorak Wines	Cabernet Sauvignon Cabernet Shiraz
Northern S.A. Murray Valley	Waikerie	Special Bin Dry Red
Northern S.A. Murray Valley	Loxton Co-op.	Cabernet Sauvignon Claret
Northern S.A. Murray Valley	Angoves	Tregrehan Claret Brightlands Burgundy
Great Western	Best	No. O Claret (without neck label)
Rutherglen/ Corowa	All Saints	Cabernet Sauvignon Cabernet Shiraz Claret (Cabernet Shiraz Blend) Pinot-Shiraz
Rutherglen/ Corowa	Buller	Rutherglen Shiraz
Rutherglen/ Corowa	Campbell	Bobbie Burns Shiraz
Rutherglen/ Corowa	Chambers	Cabernet Shiraz
Rutherglen/ Corowa	Gehrig	Cabernet Shiraz
Rutherglen/ Corowa	Graceray (Stanton & Killeen)	Moodemere Dry Red
Rutherglen/ Corowa	Morris	Durif Dry Red Shiraz

AREA	MAKER	LABEL
King Valley	Brown	Milawa Shiraz
Goulburn Valley Northern	Darveniza	Claret
Goulburn Valley Northern	Gravina	Dry Red
Goulburn Valley Central	Tahbilk Pty Ltd	Chateau Tahbilk Cabernet Shiraz
Wybong/ Sandy Hollow	Hordern	Wybong Estate Dry Red
Mudgee	Augustine	Cabernet Sauvignon Hermitage
Mudgee	Mudgee Wines	Cabernet Sauvignon Hermitage
Riverina	Calamia	Bin 29 Shiraz Private Bin Label Non repeating Number: Dry Red
Riverina	De Bortoli	Private Stock Claret
Riverina	McWilliam	Private Bin 14 Burgundy Private Bin Cabernet Shiraz Private Bin 35 Claret
Riverina	Miranda	Cabernet Shiraz
Riverina	Rossetto	Beelgara: Dry Red Cabernet Sauvignon

AREA	MAKER	LABEL
Swan Valley	Conteville	Hermitage
Swan Valley	Hewley Park	Burgundy
Swan Valley	Houghton	Blue Stripe: Burgundy Claret Cabernet Hermitage Strelley
Swan Valley	Olive Farm	Burgundy Claret
Swan Valley	Parri	Claret Burgundy Cabernet
Swan Valley	Peters	Shiraz Claret
Swan Valley	Riverside	Burgundy Claret Hermitage
Swan Valley	Sandalford	Cabernet Sauvignon Shiraz
Swan Valley	Valencia Wines	Perry Lakes: Burgundy Claret
Swan Valley	Waldeck	Cabernet Hermitage Claret

36   Classification of Australian Wines

BLENDS	MAKER	LABEL
Northern S.A. Murray Valley/ Reynella	Glenloth	Coromandel Claret
Reynella/ McLaren Vale	Glenloth	Cabernet Shiraz
McLaren Vale/ Barossa/ Coonawarra	Hardy, Thomas	Cabinet Claret
Pokolbin/ McLaren Vale	Hardy, Thomas	St Thomas Burgundy
Watervale/ Barossa Valley	Lindeman	Cawarra Claret St Cora Burgundy
Murray Valley/ Coonawarra/ McLaren Vale	Mildara	'Grove' Claret Merebin Estate Hermitage
Barossa Valley/ Angle Vale	Norman	Angle Vale Burgundy
South Australia/ Griffith/ Wybong	Penfold	Dalwood Burgundy Dalwood Claret Dalwood Hermitage
Watervale/ McLaren Vale	Quelltaler	San Carlo Claret
Barossa Valley/ Barossa Ranges	Saltram	Selected Vintage Burgundy
Great Western/ Barossa Valley/ Rutherglen	Seppelt	Chalambar Burgundy Moyston Claret
Barossa Valley/ Barossa Ranges	Stonyfell	Private Bin Burgundy
Clare/ Barossa Valley/ McLaren Vale	Woodley	Queen Adelaide Claret

BLENDS	MAKER	LABEL
Not Revealed	Wynn	Ovens Valley Shiraz
Murray Valley/ Barossa Valley	Yalumba	4 Crown Burgundy 4 Crown Claret
Murray Valley/ Barossa Ranges	Yalumba	Galway Vintage Burgundy

WHITE WINES
OUTSTANDING WINES

AREA	MAKER	LABEL
Clare/ Barossa Ranges	Leo Buring	Reserve Bin Label: Rhine Riesling Moselle Late picked Riesling
Clare	Stanley Wine Co.	Leasingham: Bin 5 Rhine Riesling Bin 6 Mosel Bin 7 Rhine Riesling Bin 3 White Burgundy Bin 9 Late Picked Rhine Riesling

Barossa Valley	Orlando	'Selected Wine'
		Rhine Riesling (coded
		  number)
		Rhine Riesling –
		  Moselle Style
		Spaetlese Riesling

Barossa Ranges	Orlando	Steingarten Rhine Riesling
Barossa Ranges	Yalumba	Pewsey Vale: Rhine Riesling Semillon

38   Classification of Australian Wines

Area	Maker	Label
Pokolbin/ Rothbury	Elliott	Tallawanta Riesling Oakvale Riesling
Pokolbin/ Rothbury	Lindeman	Hunter River (4 Number Label): Chablis Riesling White Burgundy Porphyry (sweet)
Pokolbin/ Rothbury	Rothbury Estate	Rothbury Estate Label with vineyard blocks signified e.g. A1, B2, C4
Pokolbin/ Rothbury	Tulloch	Glen Elgin Private Bin: Riesling Aucerot-Riesling
Pokolbin/ Rothbury	Tyrrell	Hunter Valley: Riesling Blanquette Shiraz Pinot Chardonnay Pinot Riesling
Hunter Flats	Elliott	Belford Riesling

WHITE WINES
VERY GREAT WINES

Area	Maker	Label
Clare	Wolf Blass	Bilyara Rhine Riesling
Watervale	Leo Buring	Reserve Bin Label denoting Rhine Riesling from Watervale Black Label:

AREA	MAKER	LABEL
		Bin 33 Riesling
		Bin 21 Moselle
		Bin 86 White Burgundy
Watervale	Lindeman	Watervale Rhine Riesling
Barossa Valley (Angle Vale)	Norman	Angle Vale White Burgundy
Barossa Valley	Orlando	'Selected Wine' Spaetlese Frontignan Chenin Blanc
Barossa Valley	Saltram	Rhine Riesling
Barossa Ranges	Hardy	Siegersdorf Riesling
Barossa Ranges	Henschke	Rhine Riesling Mosel White Frontignac
Barossa Ranges	Kaiser Stuhl	Individual Vineyard: Gold Ribbon Riesling Green Ribbon Riesling Purple Ribbon Late Picked Riesling
Barossa Ranges	Yalumba	Carte d'Or Riesling
Reynella/ Happy Valley/ Coromandel Valley	Marienberg	Rhine Riesling
McLaren Vale	Seaview	Rhine Riesling
Keppoch	Seppelt	Special Label with Code Number: Keppoch Rhine Riesling
Great Western	Seppelt	Special Label with Code Number:

AREA	MAKER	LABEL
		Great Western Rhine Riesling Other Varietal Wines e.g. Chasselas
Pokolbin/ Rothbury	Drayton	Bellevue White Burgundy
Pokolbin/ Rothbury	House of Reynell	Hungerford Hill Pokolbin Semillon
Pokolbin/ Rothbury	McWilliam	Mt Pleasant Anne Riesling
Pokolbin/ Rothbury (also Wybong)	Penfold	Special Bin: Hunter Valley Blanquette Bin 700 Hunter Valley Riesling Bin 568 Hunter Valley Pinot Riesling Bin 365
Pokolbin/ Rothbury	Pokolbin Winemakers	Semillon
Wybong/ Sandy Hollow	Hollydene	Semillon
Mudgee	Craigmoor	Chardonnay Semillon Chardonnay
Minchinbury/ Wybong/ Adelaide Environs	Penfold	Traminer Riesling Bin 202

WHITE WINES
GREAT WINES

Area	Maker	Label
Clare	Stanley Wine Co.	Stanley Riesling
Watervale	Quelltaler	Vintage Riesling
Barossa Valley	Glenview	Krondorf: Johannisberger Riesling Clare Riesling
Barossa Valley	Orlando	Barossa Riesling
Barossa Ranges	Hamilton	Eden Valley: Rhine Riesling Springton Riesling
Barossa Ranges	Hardy, Thomas	Eden Moselle
Barossa Ranges	Kaiser Stuhl	Reserve Bin Rhine Riesling
Barossa Ranges	Penfold	Eden Valley Moselle
Adelaide Environs	Hamilton	Clare Riesling Ewell Moselle
Adelaide Environs	Douglas A. Tolley	Pedare Rhine Riesling
Reynella/ Happy Valley/ Coromandel Valley	Light Wines	Rhine Riesling
McLaren Vale	Kay	Amery Rhine Riesling Amery Late picked Riesling
McLaren Vale	Southern Vales Co-op.	Rhine Riesling

42   Classification of Australian Wines

AREA	MAKER	LABEL
Coonawarra	Mildara	Coonawarra Rhine Riesling
Coonawarra	Wynn	Coonawarra Estate Rhine Riesling
Great Western	Best	No. O Hock with neck showing grape variety and vintage year
Rutherglen/ Corowa	All Saints	Lyre Bird: Riesling White Burgundy
King Valley	Brown	Milawa: Rhine Riesling, Gewurztztraminer, White Frontignac
Central Goulburn Valley	Tahbilk Pty Ltd	Chateau Tahbilk: Marsanne, Riesling
Pokolbin/ Rothbury	W. Drayton & Sons	Bellevue: Rhine Riesling
Pokolbin/ Rothbury	McWilliam	Elizabeth Riesling
Wybong/ Sandy Hollow	Hordern	Wybong Estate Riesling
Riverina	McWilliam	Private Bin Rhine Riesling
Swan Valley	Houghton	White Burgundy

BLENDS	MAKER	LABEL
Clare/ Barossa Valley	Bernkastel	Langmeil Riesling
Barossa Valley/ Barossa Ranges/ Clare	Leo Buring	Chateau Leonay: Vintage Rhine Riesling Vintage Moselle Vintage White Burgundy
Barossa Ranges/ Pokolbin	Hardy	Old Castle Riesling
Several 'Great' Areas	Lindeman	Bin 64 Chablis Bin 11 Moselle Bin 36 Porphyry (sweet) Bin 23 Riesling Bin 77 White Burgundy

WHITE WINES
VERY GOOD WINES

AREA	MAKER	LABEL
Watervale	Quelltaler	Hock Chablis Special Bin Moselle Sauternes White Burgundy
Barossa Valley	Leo Buring	Vintage Sauternes Extra Special Riesling Extra Special Moselle Liebfrauwein Rhinegolde Moselle

AREA	MAKER	LABEL
Barossa Valley	Chateau Yaldara	Rhine Riesling Moselle
Barossa Valley	Glenview	Glenview Moselle Krondorf Semillon
Barossa Valley	Kaiser Stuhl	Bin 55 Moselle Bin 44 Riesling
Barossa Valley	Karlsberg	Rhine Riesling
Barossa Valley (Angle Vale)	Norman	Angle Vale Rhine Riesling Angle Vale White Frontignac
Barossa Valley	Orlando	Miamba Riesling Miamba Moselle Miamba Chablis
Barossa Valley	Saltram	White Frontignac
Barossa Valley	Seppelt	Melita Moselle
Barossa Valley	St Hallett's	Rhine Riesling
Barossa Valley	Wilsford	Riesling
Barossa Valley	Yalumba	Koorianda White Burgundy Golden Ridge Riesling (late picking) Yalumba Hock Yalumba Sauternes
Barossa Ranges	Glenview	Krondorf: Dry Tokay
Barossa Ranges	Henschke	Sercial Ugni Blanc
Adelaide Environs	Hamilton	Verdelho Adelaide Riesling Special Reserve Sauternes

AREA	MAKER	LABEL
Adelaide Environs	Wynn	Modbury Estate: Riesling Sauternes White Burgundy Chablis Moselle Huntersfield Riesling
Reynella/ Happy Valley/ Coromandel Valley	House of Reynell	Reynella Riesling Reynella Moselle
McLaren Vale	D'Arenberg	White D'Arenberg
McLaren Vale	Dover Wine Co.	Riesling
McLaren Vale	Hardy, Thomas	Golden Nectar Sauternes
McLaren Vale	Kay	Amery Hock
Langhorne Creek	Bleasdale	Dry White Frontignac Semillon Verdelho
Northern S.A. Murray Valley	Angove's	Bookmark Riesling Nanya Moselle
Northern S.A. Murray Valley	Waikerie Co-op.	Rhine Riesling
Great Western	Best	No. O Hock (without neck label)
Great Western	Seppelt	Rhymney Chablis
Rutherglen/ Corowa	All Saints	Beverley's Blend Riesling
Rutherglen/ Corowa	Gehrig	White Hermitage

46   Classification of Australian Wines

Area	Maker	Label
King Valley	Brown	Milawa Chablis White Grenache Tokay White Hermitage
Central Goulburn Valley	Tahbilk Pty Ltd	Chateau Tahbilk: Moselle White Hermitage
Vic. Murray Valley West	McWilliam	Robinvale Lexia
Vic. Murray Valley West	Mildara	Irymple Rhine Riesling
Pokolbin/ Rothbury	Drayton	Bellevue Semillon
Pokolbin/ Rothbury/ Wybong	Penfold	Dalwood White Burgundy
Pokolbin/ Rothbury	Pokolbin Winemakers	White Burgundy
Pokolbin/ Rothbury	Tulloch	Pokolbin Riesling
Mudgee	Augustine (N.S.W.)	Semillon
Riverina	McWilliam	Private Bins: Chablis Hock Moselle Riesling Tokay White Burgundy
Swan Valley	Houghton	Blue Stripe: Chablis Riesling

AREA	MAKER	LABEL
Swan Valley	Sandalford	White Burgundy Chenin Blanc
Swan Valley	Valencia	Perry Lakes: Chablis Riesling Sauternes
Swan Valley	Waldeck	White Burgundy

BLENDS	MAKER	LABEL
Barossa Valley/ Barossa Ranges	Augustine (S.A.)	Rhine Riesling
Langhorne Ck./ McLaren Vale	Glenloth	Rhine Riesling
Murray Valley/ Happy Valley	Glenloth	Coromandel Riesling
Various Areas	Lindeman	Cawarra Riesling
Coonawarra/ Pokolbin	Mildara	Golden Bower Riesling
Coonawarra/ Vic. Murray Valley	Mildara	Merebin Estate Riesling Merebin Estate Moselle
Various Areas	Penfold	Dalwood Chablis
Various Areas	Penfold	Private Bin Sauternes Vintage Sauternes
Barossa Valley/ Barossa Ranges	Saltram	White Burgundy

48 Classification of Australian Wines

BLENDS	MAKER	LABEL
Barossa Valley/ Clare/ Great Western	Seppelt	Arawatta Riesling CB3 Riesling
Clare/ Barossa Valley	TST	Tollana Riesling Tollana Moselle
Barossa Valley/ Barossa Ranges	Woodley	Queen Adelaide Riesling

Chart showing Comparable Qualities of Australian Wines according to Regions and Years

YEAR	CLARE/WATERVALE	THE BAROSSA	SOUTHERN VALES	S.E. SOUTH AUSTRALIA	S.W. VICTORIA	N.E. VICTORIA	GOULBURN VALLEY	HUNTER VALLEY	
1973	***	***	***	****	*****	****	****	****	R
1972	****	*****	*****	*****	*****	***	***	***	E
1971	**	***	***	***	****	****	****	*	D
1970	****	****	***	****	****	****	****	*****	
1969	**	*	*	****	****	***	****	*****	W
1968	***	***	***	****	****	***	****	**	I
1967	****	****	****	****	****	****	****	****	N
1966	***	***	**	****	****	****	****	****	E
1965	****	***	**	**	**	****	*****	*****	S
1964	****	****	****	****	****	****	****	****	
1963	****	***	****	*****	***	***	***	***	
1962	*****	*****	*****	*****	***	***	****	***	
1973	****	****	****	****	***	***	***	****	W
1972	*****	*****	*****	****	*****	***	***	****	H
1971	***	**	****	***	***	****	****	***	I
1970	****	****	****	***	***	***	***	*****	T
1969	***	***	***	**	**	****	***	****	E
1968	***	***	**	**	***	**	**	****	
1967	*****	****	****	****	****	*****	***	*****	W
1966	****	****	**	NA	****	****	***	***	I
1965	*	*	*	NA	**	***	***	****	N
1964	***	****	***	NA	****	****	***	****	E
1963	***	***	**	NA	***	***	***	****	S
1962	****	*****	****	NA	***	***	***	****	

* Poor Year   ** Poor to Average Year   *** Good Year
**** Great Year   ***** Exceptional Year   NA Not Applicable

Explanation of Vintage Chart

What makes a good vintage year?

There are two ways of looking at this question. If the rains fall at the right time and the sun shines just sufficiently when it is needed and there is no frost, or hail or thunderstorms or severe winds at harvest time, then it is a good vintage year – at least as far as the vigneron is concerned. On the other hand, if the newly made wine has a perfect colour, a tremendous aroma, beautiful flavour and the right proportion of sugar, acid and tannin then, irrespective of what the weather has been, it is a good vintage year.

Ultimately, the taste and smell of a wine determines whether the year is a good one or not. In ten years time, everyone except the worker in the vineyard will have forgotten what the weather was like. Only the wine in the glass is important. It is the only thing which will tell us whether the year in which it was made was a good vintage year.

Consensus of opinion is the only criterion by which we can judge. If a majority of intelligent drinkers of some repute consider that 1961 was an outstanding year for Bordeaux reds we will have to abide by their opinion.

Nevertheless it is nearly always a matter of fact that if the weather in a particular year was perfect for grapes then the wine itself will be extremely good.

Naturally the assessment of quality in comparative years presented in this volume is based largely on my notes over the years. I have taken due cognisance of the opinions of my fellow wine men. In the end, I suppose, it is what I have thought about the wines that has been the acid test.

If this sounds egoistic, remember that I am a wine merchant, receiving and handling hundreds of different wines every month, tasting them, talking about them, recording them, recommending them, condemning them where necessary.

In the overall picture there is not very much difference in the quality of most areas from year to year. The sun shines brightly every summer. The rain falls in winter and autumn for most years. Sometimes there is a very hot summer. Sometimes there is a lot of cloud. On the whole, however, vintage variation is not great.

The exception is the Hunter Valley which I have dealt with thoroughly in chapter 7.

Len Evans has pointed out quite effectively that in a run of years of any particular wine there is rarely a continuity of style, a similarity of pattern by which you could identify the wine. This, in my opinion, is not vintage variation or variation due to weather.

My point about all this is that in ten years you are likely to find that the quality of wine from any area is very even. In any particular year one maker might be up (in quality). Another might be down. Hence in assessing the quality of a year an 'averaging out' must be done.

For example, 1969 was a fairly poor year for reds over all South Australia. At Coonawarra Wynn's had an extremely poor vintage. Their wine was thin and acid because they were caught by the rains at vintage time. Redman had a very good year and his 1969 is one of the outstanding wines of the decade. He was fortunate (or clever) in getting his grapes in before the rain. The other makers were varied, but on the whole their wine was not very much inferior to that of previous years.

We cannot, therefore, grade 1969 in Coonawarra as an 'exceptional' year because of Redman but we can grade it as 'very good' because of the average.

You will find that *** or very good is quite a common grading for most years in most districts. There has not been a significant departure from a fairly high average. The very great year or the poor year is rare.

See also explanation of areas covered by vintage chart pp. 197–8.

Introduction

Obviously no classification of wine areas anywhere in the world will be valid for more than a certain time.

No sooner has this present classification been published than it will be improved upon, re-structured, added to, subtracted from, regraded and perhaps changed beyond recognition by wine authorities who have greater powers than I.

Yet there has to be a first. It is far more difficult to do anything a first time. It is easy to improve what already exists, and change is inevitable. Some new areas will appear, some old areas will disappear. Some downgraded vineyards will perhaps prove themselves as worthy of re-assessment.

No classification, therefore, can expect to be valid for more than a limited period.

I would remind all would-be tinkerers, however, that my classification is based on vineyards, not on wineries, and vineyards last longer than winemakers.

I have deliberately avoided including a number of wines which may have been famous in an odd kind of way, the inclusion of which would only do damage to the classification. I refer to the very rare bottlings of some of the largest firms; bottlings which were oddities in the sense that they cannot be repeated in sufficient quantities to make their classification possible. The **Lindeman's Porphyry 1270** of 1956 gained something like twenty-eight gold medals and was one of the greatest Australian sweet unfortified wines we have seen. The **Penfolds 414 Sauternes** of 1962 was of similar quality.

Penfold's do not endeavour to issue a Bin 414 type of Sauternes every year nor even every five years, so we may as well forget it. Lindeman's do issue a four number Porphyry almost every year and no doubt some of them come pretty close to the 1270. Therefore it is worthwhile including the four number Porphyry in our classification.

The odd wines produced by McWilliam's from year to year and which are distributed privately are of no value to us. None of them are so exciting that you would prefer to have them to a classified Bordeaux and they are not very superior to the **Philip Hermitage** of the same company.

Penfold's odd Bin numbers of the early sixties which no longer appear on the market caused a little flurry at the time but in retrospect they did not nearly approach the quality of **Grange Hermitage** nor were they much better than **Bin 389** in most years. To mention them as desirable in the perspective of future years would be to invite derision.

The occasional ravings you see about the early **Great Western** reds and whites, the **Hardy Cabernet Sauvignon** blends from different areas which we saw in the fifties and sixties and the **Reynella** heavy Cabernets of the fifties are best forgotten. These are wines that are not made anymore and are not likely to be made. The wine world calls for something lighter and with more finesse. They deserved the praise they received in the context of the wines of those days, but we make wines today which fit in better with the great wines of the rest of the world and in sufficient quantities for them to be included in a classification.

Classification of Wines rather than Vineyards

A difficulty, which surely must be experienced even in France, is that wine from a certain classic area will vary according to the maker.

Not every wine from a great wine area is a great wine. The reason very often is that the maker does not know how to use the first class material that is available to him. It seems natural, therefore, that wines should be classified according to their makers as well as according to their districts. The quality of a wine may improve with change of ownership or even change of management. Conversely it may go downhill.

Accordingly, a classification according to winemakers and labels will be entirely variable. It may not be valid for more than five years and I would expect that a properly controlled classification would be subject to changes by the controlling authority as the situation demands.

Vineyards, on the other hand, will keep on producing for centuries as nature directs without much change. An intelligent attempt to classify vineyards should not, therefore, require major alteration for fifty years or so.

Some of our best wines are blended; some come in odd years from areas which are not considered classic. These wines nicely fit a maker/label classification.

For example, I have not thought fit to classify the Riverina as more than a 'very good' wine region. Yet McWilliam's do manage to produce a few wines in many years from here which compare favourably with wines from areas classified as great. Hence I have classified **McWilliam's** straight **Cabernet Sauvignon** and straight **Rhine Riesling** from Riverina as 'great'. Also included as 'great' are some of the blended wines of **Lindeman's** such as **Auburn Burgundy** and **Nyrang Claret**.

Explanation of the Selection of Areas

The classified areas have been made as small as possible. What point for instance would there be in classifying the State of Victoria as a first quality area when there are many areas which produce only third quality wine?

Quality wine comes from very small areas, each of which have their own mini-climate. The Medoc in the Bordeaux region, for instance, produces some of the best red wine in the world. Côtes du Blaye, on the other hand, just across the river, does not. Montrachet in Burgundy makes white wines which can fetch fifty dollars a bottle. Mercurey, about ten kilometres away is lucky to receive a dollar for its best whites.

Max Lake can command three dollars a bottle for a red he has just made at Lakes Folly in the Pokolbin Parish of the Hunter. No one is sure if wine produced from grapes grown at Jerry's Plains, also in the Hunter, will rank any higher than a wine from Griffith.

I cannot, therefore, classify 'the Hunter' as one area, nor even as two areas 'Upper' and 'Lower'. It would be better to divide it into wine areas which correspond with the shires of local government. Hence the so-called Lower Hunter would become Greater Cessnock. Even this is hardly definitive enough. Better still to use the subdivisional parish names so that the Lower Hunter becomes Pokolbin/Rothbury. This title naturally excludes vineyards at Broke and Belford. They would have to stand under their own title.

However it is not possible to use parish names since often the parish name is only used when a transfer of land is conducted and title details need to be checked. The name of the local township, therefore, becomes all important. Vineyards clustered around the little township of Great Western are entitled to carry that name. Vineyards planted twelve miles away at Ararat cannot. The terms Lower Hunter or north-east Victoria are, consequently, too broad for the purpose of classifying vineyards.

In my classification, therefore, I have tried to follow the French system. I think of classification consisting of a number of concentric circles each one smaller than the other. Hence we might classify a vineyard this way:

1. *Region:*   North-east Victoria (widest circle)
2. *Grape growing area:*   King Valley (2nd widest circle)
3. *Vineyard:*   Milawa (3rd widest circle)
4. *Grower:*   Brown Bros. (centre of circle)
   or
1. *Region:*   Hunter Valley (widest circle)
2. *Grape growing area:*   Pokolbin/Rothbury (2nd widest circle)
3. *Vineyard:*   Ivanhoe (3rd widest circle)
4. *Grower:*   W. Drayton & Sons (centre of circle)

Under this system, while the vineyard exists, the classification remains the same, irrespective of whether it is sold or not. A vineyard may be split up into two or more sections as it is in Burgundy, but it retains its name and the grower becomes the last point of identification.

I have classified a vineyard as 'outstanding' if it has a long history of outstanding wines to its credit, or is in a small area which possesses vineyards with that history.

This classification of vineyards as opposed to wineries eliminates the possibility of buying a Fordwich wine when what was really wanted was a Pokolbin, simply because the person who made the Fordwich wine happened to have a winery at Pokolbin.

Of course the name of the vineyard would have to appear on the label and the integrity of the maker would have to be above reproach.

Since every vineyard area has its own mini climate and every section of a vineyard its own micro-climate, it has been necessary for me to separate areas which geographically may be close together but climatically are likely to be quite different. Hence I have distinguished between Wybong and Sandy Hollow. Several vineyards along the Wybong Creek seem to me to share similar climatic characteristics. These would change, I have estimated, when the valley of the Goulburn (Sandy Hollow) is entered. Similarly the flat plains of the middle part of the Hunter Valley would have quite different characteristics to Wybong and Pokolbin/Rothbury both of which have many hills to break up the direct rays of the sun from morning till dusk which the vineyards on the plains must endure.

To me, Clare has a distinctly different mini-climate to Watervale. The greater height of Clare, the heavier rainfall, the steeper hills would call for a distinction between the two areas.

Obviously until wine companies place more information on the label about the vineyard where the grapes were grown, we shall never be able to have a complete vineyard classification. For instance, Penfolds must be able to

identify blocks or sections of the vineyard at Dalwood
Estate (Wybong Park). If the labels showed exactly what
vineyards produced the wine, we would soon be able to
identify the best blocks. As it is we have to be satisfied with
'Dalwood Estate – Selected Vineyards', etc.

Notes on Special Binnings

Very often you will hear of various companies which
attach importance to high quality wines which they have
made in small batches, perhaps 4·5 or 5·5 kilolitres.
The main purpose seems to be to use these for show
purposes and without question they must be successful in
this respect. From a classification point of view they have
no value. A wine that is not released generally (say only
in quantities of two thousand dozen or so) is not representative of an area nor a winery.

McWilliam's, for example, over the years have coined
a number of names and initials for wines which the public
will probably never see. Thus there are **Richard, Frederick,
Henry, Stephen, P.** and **O.P. and O. H.** They also bottle a
number of varietal wines such as **Aucerot, Montils, Rhine
Riesling** and **Traminer**.

Penfold's play the numbers game. Thus we have (or
used to have) **Pinot Rieslings 302, B539; Sauternes 216** and
414; Clarets 610 and **707** . . . all wines you cannot buy!

Seppelt's also indulge (or used to indulge) in this numbers
game. Hence you once saw **G51, H66-68, J34** and so on.

Hardy's were in it too with their **Cabernet Sauvignon**
blends from different areas.

Orlando at one stage produced a **Trockenbeerenauslese**.

The same comment applies to a number of other firms
both large and small.

Now if these special wines were really something
tremendous, far better than current runs of similar wines
from the same companies or if they were a challenge to
classified Medocs or Rhine Valley trockenbeerenauslese
wines, then it would trouble me that they were not classified

or did not receive a mention as quality wines under their own labels; but they are not.

Penfold's Grange Hermitage is far better than their private range of clarets. **McWilliam's Frederick Hermitage** of any year is not significantly greater than their **Philip Hermitage. All Saints Reserve Bin Cabernet Sauvignon** does not leave their **Lyre Bird Cabernet Shiraz** for dead. They are not, therefore, worth reckoning in our classifications.

Let them have their fun in their private tasting rooms. We are not really missing anything.

Blended Wines

It seems to me that the practice of blending wines from different areas is one of economics rather than one that derives from good winemaking theory.

The wine theorist is appalled more than anything else. He sees that in the domain of first quality wine, purity in every sense of the word is of prime importance. Even the slight impurity of mixing wines differing in texture because of their derivation from different soils and mini-climates, though in the same area, alarms him.

The wine drinker is, on the other hand, alarmed because it disturbs his concept of what is right with the world. One of the things he considers essential is that when he pays top price for a wine it should come from one area only and from the area it says on the label. It is repugnant to him to find that it comes from any other area or that it is a blend of wines from two areas, even though the label might inform him so. It just does not seem to fit in with the order of things.

From a practical point of view the practice of blending is good. If a maker has one gallon of superb wine and ten gallons of ordinary wine, it is good wine practice to lift the quality of the poor wine by adding the good wine. Thus he will be able to sell all the wine. This does not make quality wine. All it does is to make money for the wine-maker.

The mere fact that the label states the wine comes from two or more areas does not make the winemaker any more virtuous or the wine better. It is pointless. It is preferable (for those who want to feel virtuous) to say 'This is a blended wine. Therefore it is being sold more cheaply than a straight quality wine'. The wine merchant might just as well put on the label: 'Look, this is blended from two areas. One of them is outstanding so you have to pay almost as much for the wine as if it came solely from the outstanding area'.

GRANGE HERMITAGE

In 1972 Penfold's received the magnificent Francois de Castella Trophy for the most successful exhibitor in all wine classes at the Melbourne Show.

It may surprise that this was the first time that Penfold's had won this award. After the war this great company did not exhibit in wine shows at all for many years. Some of their more feline fellow traders said that this was because they were afraid to expose their wines to open competition in case their reputation should suffer. This success was, therefore, a great feather in the cap of the Penfold board.

It vindicates their policy of ensuring that their product is top grade before it is submitted to the judges, whether they be public or wine shows.

As I see it, the main and perhaps the only value of wine shows is to stimulate winemakers to produce better wines. Whether the incentive of winning show awards has been the main reason for the improvement in Penfold's wines over the past quarter of a century or not is a matter which may be debated with Penfold's production director. In the event, it does seem that, concurrently with Penfold's winning great numbers of show awards, the general standard of their table wines has improved to a remarkable degree. If that sounds like criticism of their earlier wines it is no more so than that of all other Australian wines of a former era.

I would indeed be surprised to find any opponents of a

statement that at present Penfold's produce, quantitatively, better red table wines than any other wine company.

All this improved quality flows from the great experiment of **Grange Hermitage** which began in 1951 and resulted in the appearance of the first Grange in **1952**.

The techniques of making Grange, the experience gained in producing a wine of this type and the consequent elimination of poor processing, have so shaped the Penfold organization that it is now not difficult to recognize a Penfold red simply from its style.

Grange Hermitage is a distinctive wine of a most individual kind. Although the innovators of the great wine, Max Schubert and his associates, introduced top Bordeaux chateau methods into Australian red wine making, it seems that they must have, even subconsciously, the image of a peculiarly Australian top quality wine rather than that of an imitation of a top French wine.

The oak flavour of Grange is American rather than French. The predominant grape is shiraz which is not grown in Bordeaux, although I believe that some Rhone shiraz may have been blended in with the pre-war Bordeaux on which the first Grange must have been modelled. At all events Grange today is certainly not similar to the contemporary top chateau reds of Bordeaux. It has a tremendous volume of flavour, a huge concentrate of berry on the middle palate and the marked hardness of American oak. Obviously the berries have been picked when fully ripe and the intention of the maker has been to get bigness as well as perfect balance of flavour, acid, tannins and extracts. It has none of the 'Bordeaux sweetness' on the middle palate which we see in some other South Australian reds. The consequence is that a Grange of any year is a top quality red wine of immense character, quite up to the standard of any red wine in the world but differing vastly from any made in Bordeaux or Burgogne.

To make a great wine like Grange is really a small but wealthy winemaker's task. The reality that it is made by our largest winemakers shows their dedication to the task of producing the best red in Australia. The technique cannot be used in making large quantities of wine. Hence the **Bins 389, 28, 128, 707** and **2**, although showing some of the facets of Grange, are not Grange and never will be, in any year, as good.

For their own good reasons, the Penfold production team have chosen a certain area or areas to provide the basic material for Grange, and this is a main contributing factor in the uniqueness of Grange.

Penfolds have been unwilling to divulge the source of the grapes from which Grange Hermitage is made. Statements have been made by various executives of the company which have not been free of conflict. It seems likely to me that it is, or was, a blend.

The company has given up the Grange vineyard and has retained some of its best vineyards in South Australia with Kalimna perhaps being the most suitable for quality red wine.

It would be fitting to see the name of the vineyard, the source of the new Grange, appear on the label one day.

1 Does Australia make top quality Wines?

Over the years I have been given many books and articles on wine to review but none so poignant as the one I quote below. The article was written for a newspaper and the editor was not sure whether he should publish it and asked me to read it. I advised him not to publish. Unfortunately I never found out who wrote it because the newspaper ceased publication before I returned the article. It was not signed.

I am quoting it as a realistic, if savage, view of Australian wines expressed in rare terms. The whole context of this present book really is to answer that article, to admit the truth of it, where there is truth, and to refute it where there is not.

AUSTRALIANS DO NOT KNOW THEIR WINES

One of the extraordinary characteristics of the Australian is his sensitivity to praise or derogatory remarks. Nowhere is this characteristic more clearly perceived than in the matter of wine. It must come as a great shock to the visitor from overseas to read the vast reams of nauseating praise that is heaped upon Australian wines which are quite ordinary.

Let's face it. Australia produces a few top quality wines, but on the whole, the huge bulk of its dry reds and whites are no better than vin ordinaire. The world traveller on his motoring through France, Italy, Spain, Portugal, or even South Africa, California or South America, drinks his way literally through hundreds of gallons of wine which he can neither remember, nor has any particular wish to do so. He is not conscious that any of the nationals of these countries are particularly anxious to impress him with the merits of these ordinary beverage wines.

When he comes to Australia, however, he finds that every

restaurateur, wine waiter, or suburban host is waiting with baited breath to hear him drop pearls of wisdom and appreciation for something which he no doubt will not ever remember any more than he did all the other wines.

When he picks up his Sunday paper, he will find a column devoted to Australian wines in which he sees some claret or other with a fanciful bin number attached to it instead of a name, written up as though it were the nectar of the gods. Once or twice he may be tempted to buy such a bottle, anticipating that it will be, because of its description, one of the rare wines of this world. Much to his chagrin he finds that the opposite is often the case. He is far too polite and certainly far too diplomatic to express his opinion, although in some cases he must return to his motherland, brainwashed by the extraordinary adulation that is heaped upon Australian wines by Australian wine waiters.

If he should be so unfortunate as to attend a Wine and Food Society meeting or a Beefsteak and Burgundy Club dinner as a guest, his ears will be assailed by the same monotonous repetition and raving about the same unremarkable Australian wines as he read about in his Sunday paper. He will feel inclined to clobber across the head the next idiot who says 'this Australian wine can show the rest of the world how far superior wine making is in Australia to anywhere else'.

To illustrate some of the pompous rubbish that is written about Australian wines, take this example. 'It is one of the biggest reds from Mount Pleasant for a long time – and the wine will take many years to fulfil the promise that lies in it. I believe it may hark back to some of the fabulous '47s in style, and these wines are wonderful drinking now if you are ever lucky enough to open a bottle. Since '47 there have been hail years and wet years and mild years. Some biggish wines were made in '54 and '59, and '57 was the hottest year, producing wines that have a ton of colour, body and tannin. Many of these '57s are still hard and in one or two cases, I wonder if the fruit will subside before the hardness. The early years of the '60s were light and acid and '63 was the first reasonable vintage. '64, however, was ideal for grape growing in the district and one has to look back twenty years to compare. This wine has a ton of quality. The familiar smoky nose is in abundance and I drool at the thought of what it will be like with four or five years bottle age on it.'

Drool indeed! What a lot of bloody hooey! Wonderful! Fabulous! What more is there left to say about a wine? I shudder to think of the hallucinatory heights this writer would go to if he ever had to describe a really good French Chambertin of a good year. Really, the wine he was talking about is not worth wasting words on. If you drink any of the '57s today, you will find that they are hard, worn and tarnished. How could anybody rave so much about such an ordinary wine?

Take this from the same writer. (Len Evans – *Cellarmaster's Guide to Australian Wine*). 'This wine is full of character and has lots of complexities. The predominant flavour asserting itself at present is of Coonawarra. The nose is restrained and of the green mint/peppermint (what have you: wine flavours are so hard to describe) character that we know Coonawarra by. This carries through to the flavour on the tongue and is backed by the full fruit of the Clare constituent. The Hunter part is unassertive at present. We know how this reacts. Many a time I have heard people criticise a blend for its lack of Hunter when young, to contradict themselves a couple of years later when the Hunter character develops and comes through. The 2910 has plenty of full, fruit factors, but is still elegant with plenty of finesse and delicacy'.

Good God! What now can you say about a Chateau Latour? Take a look at this. 'Bullers Claret 1965 – Rutherglen, with its great berry nose and its full, fruity palate, its suggestion of blackberry jam; but withall so very pleasant and warming. Drink it now and enjoy its generosity, its giving of all it has – bigness, fruit, richness, satisfaction – or keep it five years and see how its flowers have bloomed into a multitude of perfumes and taste flavours. Comparing these young reds is like walking into a garden and plucking different flowers at random to sniff at and admire. While the first had the distinct fragrant aroma of a Paul Scarlett rose, the second had the heavy smell of a damp copse of plum trees in full bearing'. (Dan Murphy – *Vintage Club News*).

Really! Is it worthwhile writing all this incredible number of words about wines that do not rate any more than a little plebeian red from the foothills of the Provence area in France?

You will observe that at gatherings of Australian Wine and Food Societies someone will take a worn and beaten bottle out of his cupboard at home in the strong belief that he has a first class French wine. He wraps it in brown paper, hastily conveys it in his automobile shaking hell out of it, and places it on the table in the middle of nicely matured Australian reds which

Does Australia make top q...

members have been drinking daily for the last twen...
the wines are all masked and nobody knows what they a...
stranger in the midst, full of its little bubbles of disturbed an...
emaciated flavour stands out like a sore thumb in the ocean o...
the familiar beverages which everybody has learnt to love. One...
by one, everyone stands up, having recognized the French wine,
and says how much better are the Australian wines. To do them
justice, they believe what they say; but they do not *know* what
they say.

I once knew of a character who drank wine from the same
cask every day for ten years. The older he grew, the more acetified
became the wine, but he never noticed it and when I presented
him with a first class wine, he despised it and said 'I like the wine
out of my own cask, this one is terrible'. He had, you might say,
developed a 'cellar' palate. In the same way, Australians have
developed a 'national' palate.

If you really want to know how Australian wines stand in the
good company of first class overseas wines, do the opposite to
what our Australian-wine-infatuated Wine and Food Societies
practise.

The way to measure Australian wines against world class wines
from France is to take half a dozen of the best wines of France,
Chateau-bottled, carefully matured, carefully rested before they
are presented and carefully decanted, and to pick the best
Australian wine that you can, irrespective of where it came from
or who made it and give it the same care and attention as the
others, and to put it in the midst of them. I regret to say that of
all the people present at such a tasting, you will find it difficult
to find one who will still have a word of praise for the Australian
wine. This might have been the very wine that took all the praise
the previous night by the same men drinking under the conditions
which I described above in which the French wine was the stranger.

Nowhere do wine writers let their heads go to such an extent
as they do with Hunter Valley wines. Perhaps it is because the
men of Sydney with their prejudiced and jaundiced eyes look
with favour only on the wines of this Valley and because geographically, they are more given to chatter than the sober and
calculated minds in Adelaide and Melbourne, that this un-
conscionable raving goes on. Look at this, for example. 'I share
the view of those who enjoy the wine off Belford ahead of any
other Hunter white, as a generalization. Year after year this tiny,
gravelly bit of grapeyard, south of the railway track at Belford

---

alate for a French-
in an Australian.
too unimportant
of expressing the
different, are the

...Sy...
e Ba...
...iable p...

...of my infor...
, it is my op...

...dence that is giv...
...ersonal criticism, ...
...s make top quality
...ith the outstanding
...country. It does not
...wines equivalent to
...of France.

...n I listen to jingoistic
...r tables that an old
...mple, overshadows a
...cumstances and among
... The danger lies in the
...superior to the famous.
...might conceivably agree
...ve, five hundred million
...he world would certainly
...rvation.

...ality wines are based on
...f Europe and the Americas,
...y as it may appear, seem
...of Australia are far more
...k the Americans are from us.
...t about entirely because of
...tant though this soon will be.
...e it is our duty to be concerned
...ot so long ago, an Australian
...asily in Europe by the clothes
...future he will not be recognized

---

vines which taste
refore we should
ake wines which
e are just as out
it.

wine, as a case
l wines with an
d perhaps just

dry-as-a-bone,
d not draw an
can palate. At
is condemned
alate'. Palates,
hould learn to

ult. When all
ising line is:
ink the wine
s, 'we'll give

are our best
. Naturally,
am slowly
ns I respect
ralian wine

me explain
e areas in
very great
lass wines.
the palate

...ued wine, fabulous, almost fluorescent, b...
...o Buring is the greatest year of this vin...
of it, followed by 1946 but Doug Elliot's...
look like staying the course. And what incred...
and flavour!' (Max Lake – *Classic Wines of A*...

This uninhibited adulation of Hunter Valle...
influenced the major wine companies of Austr...
think that it is a compliment to wine simply to place...
'Hunter Valley', irrespective of whether the wine is...
from this revered area or not. Take a look at this label. 'Li...
Special Reserve Claret Bin 2565 Vintage 1963'. Then...
'This wine was vintaged from red hermitage grapes gro...
Lindeman's vineyards in the Hunter River Valley, Coonawa...
and Clare'. It is significant that the following years of this win...
or similar to it, are labelled with the sub-heading 'Hunter River,...
Coonawarra, Clare Blend'. Somebody must have taken a poke...
at them.

However, the same old thing goes on. Anybody who has a...
those magic words on the label, even if he is bringing the wine...
vineyard in Hunter Valley is anxious to get what he thinks are...
from South Australia. Hell! Who cares? Most wine-discerning...
people know that a stack of Hunter Valley wines is not worth...
a cracker and that as regards quantity, far more medium class...
wine is produced in South Australia than in the South of France.
Why make a fetish of something that simply is not true?
Have you ever read the columnists in English papers when
they describe their jaunts around Europe, or even their occasional
dinners at the best restaurants in England? Do they rave about
best European wines as our writers rave about Australian wines?
What has got into us? Are we still so juvenile that we have to
shout at every visitor that we have the best harbour, the best
sheep, the best cattle, the most beautiful women that can be seen
on the beaches in any part of the world and the best wines in the
world? Wake up Australia. It is time you travelled around a bit.

Well, first of all I admit that even the best of Australian
wines appear inferior in the presence of the best chateau
bottled wines of France. At this stage of our development
we do not have a range which compares with Chateau
Latour or Chateau Mouton Rothschild. These are in fact

---

by the wines he condemns. A national p...
man is forgivable. It is painful to see...
We are too remote, far too small and fa...
in a wine sense to indulge in the luxury...
opinion that our wines, though they are...
best in the world.

In most wine areas we cannot make w...
like French reds or German whites. Ther...
not try to. We should, though, try to m...
are like them in style. If we do not, then w...
of fashion as if we were wearing a 1950 su...

World wide fashion in making white...
in point, is for light, refreshing, low-alcoho...
abundance of fruit in the middle palate a...
a trace of sweetness running through.

Too often do I hear lavish praise of a...
fruit-lacking Australian white which would...
'Ah!' from the most sophisticated Americ...
the same time a pleasant, fruity Alsatian...
with remarks such as 'too sweet for my pa...
nevertheless, are trained and perhaps we sh...
train them better in Australia.

Obviously our winemakers are not at fa...
is said and done, their established advert...
'don't drink what you think you ought; dr...
you like'. Expressed in another way, that i...
you what you want'.

My self appointed task in life is to find what...
Australian wines and tell the world about ther...
this is not a task to be undertaken alone...
selecting a band of wine experts whose opini...
and which are respected by most of the Aus...
world.

Now, after that declaration of policy, let...
that I fully believe that there are many win...
Australia, neither a long way south nor at a...
height, which produce, in their own way first c...
A full bodied, richly flavoured, heavy on...

McLaren Vale Hermitage might taste like no other wine on earth and yet Australians love it, seek it out and would in many cases drink it in preference to any other wine. Taken on its own it is a most attractive wine which, eventually, we may be able to persuade overseas drinkers to accept with relish.

A similar wine is made around Rutherglen, Wahgunyah, Corowa and Taminick in north-east Victoria. Although it is not a virtue to acclaim that, 'no other wine is made like this in the whole world', that is the truth. Its merit lies both in that fact and that it appeals to Australians. Similarly, perhaps, the Australian opal is like no other stone in the whole world. Yet it is still regarded as outstanding in its own right.

My task is to find not only Australian top class wines which would even now be accepted on a world wide basis, but also Australian wines which, though different, are likely to be accepted in the long term as world standard. I must leave my beloved southern districts such as Coonawarra and Great Western and look further afield to places like the Swan Valley, Qualco and the Riverina. If we have formed opinions about these regions, it may be that now is the time to have a re-assessment of them. We shall find that they are not, generally speaking, in the same class as wines from the southern areas, but are of a high enough standard to be classified as 'very good'.

A General Assessment of Australian Wines

Since Australia produces a complete range of wines from aperitive to dessert, a discussion on their merits relative to the great wines of the world would seem pertinent. We seem destined never to loom large on the scene with wines labelled sherry, vermouth or port. This is undoubtedly, not because we make inferior wines of this nature to those made by the French, Italians or Spanish, but because they are sufficiently different in style to make comparison with the European products odious. Perhaps one day our aperitive and dessert wines will be regarded highly in their own right and under their own distinctive titles. For example, our ports are among the most palatable and attractive sweet red wines in the world but they simply do not taste like the port of Portugal and cannot, therefore, be compared with them.

It is in the fields of red, white and pink table wines, and champagne that Australia's light shines.

Our top quality wines of these styles compare favourably with the top wines of any other country and, in some cases, can easily be mistaken for them.

CHAMPAGNE

It is contended by the French and sometimes by other nations that we should adopt other names for our wines and abandon the European titles we adopted a hundred and fifty years ago. With the French hardening their attitude to the use of the word 'champagne' it seems that export markets will be closed to us unless we do find another name for this sparkling wine; but what? I can think of no better name than Mousseux.

Already we have changed to the American system of using grape varietal names for our table wines. Hence we use Cabernet Sauvignon, Shiraz and Pinot for our reds and Rhine Riesling, Semillon and White Hermitage for our whites.

Vintage years do not trouble us as much as they do in Europe. Not every year is a great year but then, on the other hand, there are very few poor years. Our tremendous development of technology and modern equipment tends to iron out differences of years and almost makes true our boast that 'every year is a vintage year'.

When I recommend wines I take care to mention that I refer only to the top quality lines of any maker, certainly not to his whole range.

In sparkling wines we scintillate, but then only spasmodically. In **1953 Seppelt's Great Western Champagne** gained first prize against all comers at an exhibition held in

California – definitely a shock for the French exhibitors. **Great Western Brut champagne** with a year on the label – commonly known as 'Vintage Brut' could take on all comers still and no doubt occasionally collect first prize; but it is rare and expensive. I would doubt that any but the most skilled of champagne connoisseurs could pick it in a line up of the best champagne of the world.

Other Australian champagnes can be good. They are not great. They will not be great until we use the pinot grape in their make-up. The best of them are **Penfold's Minchinbury**, **Romalo**, **McWilliam's** and **Hardy's**. Seppelt's put out a champagne of similar quality to these. It is simply called **Great Western Imperial**.

WHITE WINES

Australian white wines are divided into two classes – rieslings (or wines of great firmness, lightness of body and pleasant tartness) and full bodied whites (or wines of generous texture, lacking slightly in acid). The best rieslings are made from grapes grown in the cooler areas of South Australia and Victoria. A slightly sweet riesling often carries the name 'Moselle' (or Mosel). A 'late picked' riesling is very often, but not necessarily, sweet.

The full bodied whites appear under the names of white burgundy, chablis or grape varietal names such as semillon, palomino, white hermitage or traminer. Most viticultural areas of Australia produce this style.

No Australian white is like a German wine. The rieslings, in their own way, are among the most beautiful wines in the world. The best of them are very pale in colour, crisp, have a beautifully perfumed bouquet, a wonderfully fruity centre palate and a finish which is sustained to the end. The South Australian rieslings together with Hunter Valley white burgundy styles are our best white wines. Their quality is immediately obvious and when one becomes accustomed to their dryness they may be enjoyed far more than the sweeter wines of Germany. Occasionally a sweet 'late picked' riesling is confused with a 'spaetlese' or 'auslese' Rhine wine.

Our best rieslings are marketed under the name of
Leasingham, **Orlando**, **Yalumba**, **Buring**, **Kaiser Stuhl**,
Hardy, **Coonawarra**, **Seaview** and **McWilliam**.

The full bodied whites have a similar character to many
other wines of the world – notably the bigger bodied wines
of France, the wines of Northern Italy, the Rioja area of
Spain, South Africa and California. There are many
occasions when a well known connoisseur, given a masked
bottle, has hesitated between naming an Australian wine
as a Mersault or a Hunter Valley white. On other occasions
there seem to be similarities with white Bordeaux or
Orvieto wines.

We have more top quality full bodied white wines than
we do rieslings. The best of them, made in the Hunter
Valley, have a strong pleasant bouquet, a full rich centre
palate and leave a splendid flavour on the tongue after
consumption. **Lindeman**, **McWilliam**, **Penfold**, **Drayton**,
Elliott, **Tulloch**, **Rothbury Estate** and **Reynell** produce
outstanding Hunter whites of this nature. In South Australia, **Orlando**, **Buring**, **Leasingham** and **Wynn** make
excellent examples. **Seppelt's** make superb white wines of
this class at Great Western in Victoria.

RED WINES

Our red wines are firm and austere, or soft and full. The
firm reds tend to approximate the wines of Bordeaux,
the cabernet wines of California and South Africa or
perhaps, on occasions, a Hungarian or Yugoslav red.
The softer wines are sometimes similar to the Rhône Valley
wines of France, at other times to those of Piedmont in
Italy, occasionally like those of Rioja and very often like
the fuller reds of California.

The technique of using new oak for the pre-bottle
maturing period gives a superficial likeness to Bordeaux
wines which the connoisseur readily learns to recognize.
The reds of Coonawarra treated in this manner are not so
easily distinguished and many a top wine man has been
embarrassed in finding he has named a Coonawarra red

as a premier cru Medoc when it has been presented to him masked.

The best Coonawarra reds are those of **Redman, Penfold, Lindeman, Mildara, Brand** and **Wynn**. A multitude of top ranking firm reds are available in small quantities besides these.

Penfold's Grange Hermitage, Orlando Cabernet and **Orlando Hermitage, Seppelt's Great Western** reds, **Hardy's Cabernet, Seaview Cabernet, Kaiser Stuhl** reds, **Wolf Blass Cabernet, Tahbilk** reds and **Brown Bros.** reds are (in good years) examples of our best firm styles.

As with the whites the Hunter Valley produces the best softer style reds. **Penfold, Lindeman, McWilliam, Elliott** and **Tulloch** are the master makers in this field. **Dr Max Lake** makes a unique red which has a great deal of oak character and does not fit easily into any style. It is a classic wine in its own right. **Rothbury Estate** and **Reynell** (in the Hunter) are newcomers to the field and their wines need ageing before we know what their quality will be like. **McWilliam's** make beautiful soft reds at Griffith in New South Wales.

The north-east Victorian reds are even more full bodied than the average soft reds of Australia, although there is a great similarity between these and the reds of McLaren Vale in South Australia. They may perhaps be described as traditional Australian style wines, being heavy, full of fruit, soft and with plentiful flavour. **All Saints, Brown Bros., Bailey, Booth** and **Chambers** are the names to remember for this type of wine from Victoria. **Hardy, Ryecroft, Osborn** and **Kay** are the McLaren Vale makers to keep in mind for this style of wine.

There are many other Australian dry table wines of varying styles that are of a fairly high standard. It is true that there is no poor Australian wine but, apart from those I have mentioned above there are none, perhaps, that are worth remembering any more than average wines from any other country.

Rosé wines

Australian rosé style wines vary tremendously from the semi-sweet Portuguese styles to the dry Rhône Valley styles of France. **Seppelt's Spritzig Rosé** and **Kaiser Stuhl Rosé** have proved the most popular in the Portuguese style and **Hardy's Mill Rosé** is possibly the best in the French style. They certainly are attractive wines and deserve more attention than they receive.

It can be seen from the preceding that I believe Australia *does* indeed make top quality wines whether they be aperitive, dessert, sparkling or table wines such as claret, riesling or rosé. However, in this book we shall be dealing only with red and white table wines.

2 What is a Top Quality Wine Area?

Obviously a top quality wine area is one from whence come outstanding wines. Faced with the task of selecting the outstanding wines of Australia, the first question to be answered is, 'what criteria should be used?'.

It would be the height of egotism and indeed futility for any man to claim that he, and he alone, was the sole determining authority in the matter, even in the circumstances where he had a solid following. Andre Simon in England was probably the closest ever to the position of being a single authority on the excellence of the wines produced or sold in a country. Alexis Lichine, for a time at least, was regarded as America's lexicon of wine.

Yet both these authorities relied absolutely on well established paths. Not for them the high wire of naming new countries, nor even new areas in old countries. It was Bordeaux and Burgundy which they set up as the norms of quality for red wine. Their dictums in the long run were only advice on what was good from those two areas for any particular year.

Luigi Veronelli holds the position of greatest authority on wines in Italy; but he takes no risks with his reputation. No doubt his favourite wines are Piedmontese, but he has a favourable word for every named wine in the country. It is instructive, however, to observe his remarks on the work he has done in listing (but not classifying) Italian wine. He says, 'Once in possession of the bottle, drink the wine respecting my advice and compare your judgements with mine. I have given it after many samples collected and examined throughout the course of the years. I want to stress that I have not come to a judgement of averages, but have confirmed as valid the one taken from the best samples, even if they were not the most numerous'.

This is an interesting policy which we shall have to investigate further during the course of this book. I intend, you see, to undertake a thorough analysis of the wines of Australia for the purpose of finding out which are the best.

This may lead us into strange parts, for wine making techniques are more capable now of converting grapes once considered suitable only for average quality wine into first class beverages capable of being compared with the best of other regions. The techniques are expensive and require the intensive care of highly paid chemists.

Nonetheless, our main difficulty is to be – upon whose judgement are we to rely when it comes to selecting the outstanding wines of this country? We have no long history of wine drinking to help us; no areas of quality, established beyond doubt; no tradition at all, so it appears, when it comes to deciding our best wines.

Certainly we have many men's opinions, but these are diverse. We have the extravagant praise of the winemakers concerning their own products, but this is scarcely acceptable as a criterion of quality.

We have the added complication that 'outstanding wines' might be not only red and white table wines, but should include the possibility of our sweet table wines like sauternes, or of our so-called ports and sherries, sparkling wines, muscats, tokays and other dessert wines.

We are obliged, if we follow practices of countries with existing wine reputations, to understand the expression 'outstanding wines' as meaning in fact 'outstanding wine districts' rather than individual wines under some particular label or other. This is likely to be a contentious interpretation since it excludes blended or 'cellar' wines. Max Lake in his excellent publication, *Classic Wines of Australia*, includes very many blended wines which he considers and are, indeed, first class. Yet the point is crucial. Australia must present to the world a list of districts about which it can say 'These districts produce, under ideal conditions of weather and winemaking, the outstanding wines of this country. Just as Bordeaux and Burgundy present the best red and white wines of France; Piedmont, the best of Italy; the Middle Rhine and its tributaries, the best of Germany; the Rioja and Jerez, the best of Spain; and the Duro Valley, the best of Portugal, so do these areas outlined above present the best of Australian wines.'

I attempted to define a top quality wine in my book *Australian Wine – The Complete Guide* (Chapter 21): 'An outstanding wine must have all the features of a good mature wine in a more remarkable way. With every nosing there must be a new pleasure. With every mouthful there will be an effusion of different and delightful sensations. It must be a wine which lives in the memory of experienced wine lovers and about which they will sigh from time to time.'

The more wine I drink and the more I discuss wine matters with our wine chemists the more I am convinced that wine quality is closely related to a fairly cool summer temperature and a long ripening period for the grapes. Good winemaking can overcome many of the defects of a too hot climate, but when the dividends are handed out it will be found that it is easier and more profitable to make quality wine from grapes grown in naturally cool conditions than in warmer regions.

Before we can obtain a true picture of why some wines are as good as they are, it is necessary to know something of the physiology of the vine.

The grape vine is an individualist in the plant world. It takes its own time with bud burst which does not correspond with that of similar plants. It has its own cycle of development from bud burst to final cropping and each variety of grape is different in this respect. This cycle is dependent on the nature of each particular vine and on the pattern of climate. We should examine how a vine plant grows and produces fruit.

All substances that enter the vine roots from the soil must be in a water solution. Mineral nutrients for the vine are salts and their ions. Absorption into the root cell system of any particular vine depends on its cellular respiration process. The rate of accumulation of ions is closely correlated with the rate of respiration.

The rate of absorption is also dependent on the availability of sugars and readily utilizable carbohydrates in the roots. In addition, the root cells have the ability to absorb some ions in much greater quantity than others. For example, potassium and nitrates are absorbed several times as rapidly as calcium, magnesium and sulphate. Thus the presence of a dissolved ion in the soil solution does not necessarily mean it will be absorbed by the roots.

The main factors relating to absorption are *transpiration* and *photosynthesis*. These are directly related to the sunlight and the sun's heat. The same vine planted in similar soils only a few miles apart will react quite differently according to the amount of light and heat it receives. Hence I make my point that the correct grape variety and a perfect climate are far more important in producing perfect wine than the soil factor.

The maker of first class wine is seeking to grow grapes which at vintage time are firm, with a good balance of sugar and acid, filled with juice and with a pleasing and rich aroma and flavour. When he tastes the grapes he expects them to have a zesty flavour. When he chews the skins he expects a tannin rasp on his tongue which tastes clean and strong. He wants his grapes to be ready for picking not only with the right sugar/acid ratio but to be fairly small for the variety, neat and tightly packed and in a fully filled tight and graceful bunch. If his grapes are too big the distribution of flavour elements will be too dispersed to make a tasty, highly select wine.

He does not particularly care if his soil is sandy, gravelly, of slate or of chalk or even if he grows his vines in a field of cotton wool, as long as it is well supplied with water and it feeds his vines with the necessary mineral salts through its root system.

The perfect vine is one that possesses an equitable

balance between root growth and leaf surface. Given a soil with a good supply of water to its roots and a supply of the necessary minerals, the vine will grow well but it will not necessarily produce perfect wine.

For quality grapes the vigneron needs a precisely suitable environment.

Transpiration is the replacement of the losses of water from the green parts of the vine, especially from the leaves. The rate of water loss is dependent largely on the external conditions of light intensity, temperature, humidity and wind.

Photosynthesis (from the Greek word *photo* for light) is the process whereby the vine manufactures its food in the leaves. Light performs several functions in relation to the vine. It produces sugars, proteins and fats. It uses its energy to split water and release oxygen. The hydrogen remaining from the split water is combined with carbon dioxide, derived from the air, to form carbohydrates.

The grower of quality grapes, therefore, needs an exact climate for producing quality grapes. Light from the sun must be sufficient to effect, at the right time, photosynthesis in the leaves. The rain must fall mostly in the winter and spring so that development of the vine and its greenery will be satisfactory and the development of the berries will be steady. Too much rain in summer and autumn will damage the grapes and encourage fungous disease. If the rain is heavy at vintage he may lose his crop and his pickers may not be able to get into the vine-yards. He must have a slow increase in heat from the warmth of spring to the intensity of midsummer. This brings on a steady increase in transpiration with equal growth in root structure and green leaves, top wood and shoots. Root growth under these conditions becomes acclimatized to the demand for more and more water as the weather becomes warmer.

The grower desires a slow ripening process with a slow development of sugars and flavours and a slow lessening of acidity. He wishes to harvest in the autumn when the weather is cool and the grapes have reached a satisfactory degree of sugar content but while the acid is still fairly high. Undoubtedly other areas besides Coonawarra exist in Australia which possess climatical conditions similar to those I have described. It is my contention, however, that at this point of time it is the only Australian wine area of any size which produces them precisely and consistently.

Obviously mean summer temperature is related to latitude, altitude and proximity to the sea. For the purpose of the maker of quality wine, it is not a matter of the mean temperature of the hottest month, for the question that must be answered is, not how hot it gets in one month, but how cool it stays throughout all summer months. However it is usual that if the hottest month shows a higher mean temperature in one particular area than others, the preceding months will also be hotter and hence the ripening of the grapes will be faster.

The exception seems to be that in the more southern areas of Australia autumn shows higher temperature readings than in places further north which have had a hotter summer. Heywood, for example, usually has a higher March temperature than Great Western, sixty miles further north. I find it interesting that the Upper Hunter has a lower mean summer temperature than Pokolbin. The mean temperature of the hottest month at Muswellbrook is 22°C and of Pokolbin, 23.9°C. Perhaps we shall see higher quality wines coming from this new area.

Despite the amazing quality of the soft warm wines produced in the Hunter, my preference is for the firmer wines of the south and I believe that our greatest wines will come from areas 35°S or more, or, if further north than this, at altitudes which will offset the greater heat natural to regions of lower latitude.

Avoca (Victoria) falls within my quality limits. It has a latitude of 37°6S and is about 1400' above sea level at Chateau Remy where the largest vineyard is situated.

This is not very much different from Great Western about sixty-four km to the south-west but Chateau Remy is advancing up the slopes of the jutting bulk of Mt Avoca and the air sliding down the mountain in the spring disperses the devastating frosts which worry the Great Western vignerons.

Coonawarra has the same troubles with frost because here the land is so flat and the air so still that the vines are frozen before the alarm bells have got the vineyard workers out of bed. A little to the north of Coonawarra at Keppoch a low range of hills helps the movement of air, but apparently not enough as the 1970/71 season saw a disastrous frost which wiped out every sprouting bud. Fortunately a secondary crop saved the day.

At all events, Avoca which Remy Martin of France and Nathan and Wyeth of Australia began as a brandy making venture, seems destined to be making top quality wines and the owners will probably change their minds about the eventual fate of their grapes. After all there is more money in first class wine than in brandy.

The grapes are picked in late April (as against February in the Hunter) and some reds are gathered in May. The sugar is 10 Baume and the acid 7 grams per litre.

A red made from 30 per cent cabernet, 40 per cent shiraz, some malbec and pinot noir, was slightly violet in colour and not very dense; but the body of the wine was sufficiently full. There was no trace of oak but it was fully flavoured and had good grip, enough to convince that the area can, if permitted, produce some of our finest quality wine.

Wine men constantly ponder the question, 'are our grape varieties best suited to our areas?' We see magnificent wine produced from shiraz in the Hunter, at Tahbilk, Great Western and Coonawarra. This is almost unbelievable when you examine the range of climate experienced by all these districts.

One wonders, however, how much greater our wines could be if we planted varieties exactly suited to the area.

Quite a deal of experimental planting has been engaged in already. Cabernet sauvignon and rhine riesling have been tried in the Hunter Valley. As these are early ripening varieties some vignerons doubt the wisdom of this procedure.

Murray Clayton, former Experimental Officer for Seppelt's, has explained that the approach in Europe has been, from long experience, to match varieties to districts. Hot area varieties are matched to hot areas and high quality wines may be made under these conditions. Murray has arrived at the conclusion that a long maturation or ripening period is desirable, finishing off with a burst of heat to bring the berries to full fruity ripeness. It would be a mistake, therefore, to grow cabernet sauvignon and rhine riesling in hot climates because they would ripen too quickly and their natural flavour would be lost. Similarly it would be foolish to plant trebbiano in a cool area because the possibilities are that, being a late ripening variety, it probably would not develop full maturity in most years.

Murray Clayton gives an example of what happens to shiraz when grown in different areas of Australia. Shiraz and semillon are mid season ripeners and hence have been fairly successful over the whole continent. Nonetheless Murray says 'If one takes shiraz and plants it in a range of climates, e.g. at the Hunter, Rutherglen, Great Western, Keppoch, Coonawarra and Drumborg there is a broad trend from lighter bodied, soft, quick ageing style in the Hunter, to the bigger, longer living style of Rutherglen, to probably the best balance at Great Western, to the acid, but full flavoured wines of Coonawarra and Drumborg.

Broadly, there is an increase in flavour and body as we pass from the hotter to the cool. Acid becomes more pronounced but it is softer.'

The difficulty faced by the vignerons is that there is no exact comparison of districts. If there were he could take an already successful top grade area as his example and plant the same grape varieties in exactly similar climatic conditions.

The vigneron must watch three main factors: heat summation or the sum of the mean daily temperature above 10°C; the average total number of sun hours and the pattern of the hottest month. Although Coonawarra and Bordeaux are similar in many respects, Murray Clayton points out that while Bordeaux has a heat summation of 2600 it has only 1385 sunshine hours compared with Coonawarra's 1560 sunshine hours but a heat summation of 2200. In other words, he says, when the sun is out in Bordeaux it is hotter on the average than at Coonawarra.

One can understand, then, why Seppelt's are evaluating about eighty grape varieties in each of eight areas. This involves the study of the vine's growth, the ripening of its fruit and the making of the wine from each variety. That is the way to discover what variety to plant in any particular area.

One puzzling aspect about the huge new plantings by both old experienced wine companies and unfledged syndicates is the almost reckless enthusiasm that has gone into planting specialized grape varieties all over the country such as cabernet sauvignon.

Murray Clayton remarked that it is not so much the selection of a quality wine area that is important as the selection of a grape variety which in a particular area will produce a quality wine.

Cabernet sauvignon, for example, is a quality grape in Bordeaux but it is not considered by French vignerons to be suitable to Burgundy. Pinot noir produces a superb wine in the Côte d'Or of Burgundy but not in Bordeaux; nor for that matter in Burgundy south of the Côte d'Or, where the gamay variety makes a far better wine. Yet gamay is so poor in the Côte d'Or that no wine made from this variety can be sold as an 'appellation controllé' wine from this area. If these are the facts in France, where winemakers have had thousands of years experience, why are our grape growers so careless about possibly wasting thousands of acres of vineland with an unsuitable variety?

The Hunter Valley has already undergone a period when all the vignerons pulled out every variety except semillon and shiraz. This indicated that they had proved to their own satisfaction the unsuitability of all types they had planted except these two. Perhaps semillon and shiraz are not the perfect varieties exactly suited to the Hunter, but to this date they have produced the Hunter's best wines in satisfactory quantities and, by and large, fairly consistently.

Why then this sudden splurge of planting large areas with pinot noir, cabernet sauvignon, malbec and merlot? We do indeed tend to become carried away with the thought that clonal selection, vine improvement and the conquering of many wine viruses have now made the arguments about the unsuitability of certain varieties in the past untenable. In my view, it does not lessen the argument that certain varieties are suited perfectly to some districts and are most unsuited to others.

Seppelt's, I notice, have been very cautious in this respect. They have been almost ultra conservative in adhering to the proved variety, shiraz, in their Great Western, Barossa Valley and Keppoch plantings. Their experimental plots of many different varieties at Great Western, Drumborg, Qualco, Rutherglen and Barooga have been very small. One cannot but be impressed with the results of some of these experiments. The pinot noir and pinot meuniere at Great Western seem to me to be, in spite of their lightness of colour, almost equal to the best burgundies of France. Contrariwise, I have not been impressed with their cabernet sauvignon wines produced at Keppoch but this could be because the vines are still young and cabernet, of all vines, needs some years before it shows its quality; nor did I consider their malbec grown at Qualco of great quality although the same reasoning might be applicable.

It is odd that the all purpose shiraz grape which makes the great, rich wines of the Hunter should also be the variety from which we make the firm, spicy wines of

Coonawarra and the complex and magnificent Grange Hermitage at Magill. Perhaps it will eventually be proved that shiraz is the perfect grape for every Australian district. At all events, it does not, in view of our experiences, seem wise to oust it just yet in favour of cabernet, malbec, merlot or pinot noir.

In the final analysis a great crop of cabernet, wherever it is grown, cannot produce too bad a wine. The dictum 'horses for courses and grapes for districts' is good philosophy and current thinking wherever wine is made.

OPINIONS OF OUR BEST WINE MEN

In determining the great wines of Australia we must take cognisance of the opinions of our best wine men, of the results of the wine shows and the conclusions of our best wine writers.

It may be contended, perhaps, that the opinion of English, American or European wine experts may be a guide as to our best wines. I could never agree to such a proposition. These authorities simply do not know enough about our wines, and almost every analysis I have heard or seen from overseas has been so remote from the facts as to invite derision.

The Australian wine man knows his own wines well; the wine shows present the best of all our makers' cellars and our wine writers are thinkers, and take a broader view of the subject of wine than one who is deeply immersed in it (figuratively) solely as a producer or wine judge. Our professional wine men have differing points of view which are sometimes related to their commercial interests. Max Lake and Murray Tyrell are probably as unbiased as any winemakers; yet one can see a strong leaning towards Hunter Valley wines in all their pronouncements. It may be simply because they like them so much.

Picking our best wine men is almost as difficult as picking our best wines. For both tasks it is very much a matter of opinion.

At least it is easier to select our best wine writers, for they are fewer. At all events, a good wine writer is also a good wine authority. If I choose a group of wine writers as representative of sound theorists of Australian wine I might be choosing unwittingly those with whom I agree or who agree with me. Ultimately, then, I shall be found guilty of making a list of Australia's outstanding wines, using my own, and not others', judgement.

But first, let us consider the wine writers individually. Some write columns for daily newspapers; some write for national magazines and some write books. Wine writers are not judged on their literary style. Rightly or wrongly, I consider that most of our best wine writers are represented in the excellent production called *The Epicurean*, and I confess to a dependence on it for gaining a knowledge of what our wine men are thinking.

Ian Hickinbotham is an eonologist and a sound, clear thinking, logical and keen researcher. Douglas Seabrook, with perhaps a wine judge's and wine merchant's point of view, is knowledgeable, indeed erudite, and accurate. Jack Ludbrook, whose articles I see too rarely, is alert, factual and a mine of information. Len Evans is terse, succinct, consistent and credible. Max Lake is learned, original, scientific and brilliant. Of course, when we talk of wine scientists, Bryce Rankine is the first and foremost, but then he writes for the professional winemaker rather than the amateur. Walter James, the best stylist of them all, deals out witty, shrewd common sense. Oscar Mendelsohn approaches wine as a chemist and is intolerant of woolly wine talk. Kevon Kemp has a point of view very similar to mine. I think he is sound, knowledgeable and clear thinking. There follows Johnnie Walker, Frank Margan, Frank Doherty, Sam Benwell, Cyril Pearl and Douglas Lamb, all honest, sincere writers, each with a point of view on wine. I am willing to glean something from all of them.

OPINIONS OF OUR PROFESSIONAL WINEMAKERS

In our search for the outstanding wines of Australia it is important to include the winemakers themselves as a source of information.

Usually, the winemaker, especially the small one, is too pre-occupied in bending over his fermenting vat to worry about outstanding wines from other countries and how they compare with ours.

Cyril Henschke might be an exception to this generalization. In 1970 he was granted a Churchill Fellowship which enabled him to make a study of German methods of viticulture and white winemaking at the Staatliches Weinbar Institut in the Rhine Valley.

Henschke whites, readily accepted as among the best in Australia, are highly distinctive. The winery has no 'pressure' tanks or totally enclosed stainless steel 'cold' fermenters. Cyril prefers to adhere to the older method of fermenting in concrete vats. He has formed the opinion that the amount of fruit flavour found in German wines is due to viticultural methods, for example, the method of training the vine and the siting on the correct slope facing the rising sun. He thought he might find the ideal position in the hills near his winery.

Mr Henschke has the reputation of a white winemaker but feels that the new varieties being planted will have the biggest influence on the quality of his reds in the future.

The Henschke reds are lighter and less astringent than many of the reds seen on the Australian market today. This puts him offside with the large national companies, who are tending to give greater fullness of flavour to their red wines with a considerable presence of oak tannin. I asked him if he believed in the method of using completely new small oak casks for the first ageing of red wine. He answered that he preferred to use casks of 100 to 300-gallon size made of oak, and that he considered they could give enough oak extract for twenty years. 'Well, then, do you admire Grange Hermitage?' I asked. 'Yes', he replied 'but the wood is a bit overdone in it'.

He considered that the cost of using new small oak casks every year was too great. This may indeed be true for mass production, but I could not consider this a valid reason for not using the Bordeaux method for producing outstanding wines of the Bordeaux style. A 300-gallon oak cask might impart some oak flavour to a wine after it had been used for five years or more, but it would not give more than a fraction of the oak character extracted from completely new 40-gallon casks as used by the Bordelaise.

Yet there is no doubt that Cyril Henschke's reasoning is true – new oak is not needed to make a first-class wine.

In determining the outstanding wines of Australia, the role of the winemaker is almost primary. He is expected to lead public tastes by the wines he makes. It is within his power to make wines of different styles, claret, burgundy or Chianti style, German Rhine style or Chablis style.

Wine judges, wine philosophers and wine writers may advise the winemaker on what style of wine to produce. They may advise the consumer what to buy. Ultimately, though, it is the winemaker who has control. If he does not want to make the wine these people outside his winery tell him to make, there is no point in arguing. The wine drinking public will drink what he makes and so he influences their palates far more than anyone else.

When it comes to fashioning an image for his country's wines, therefore, the winemaker is all powerful. He knows his power and there are times, unfortunately, when he uses it arbitrarily.

The theories of wine spokesmen not involved with the production side of the industry often appear to be ridiculed by the inner circle of executive-type winemakers of the large companies. Regrettably, either because of company policy or because they are inarticulate outside their profession, the industrial winemakers are unable to express their opinions publicly. I certainly do not criticise them for this. They are responsible for their company's profits. They will endeavour, consequently, to make the wines they think will sell best. They will also make some which they think will obtain gold medals at the various wine shows. These incentives will not, necessarily, result in all cases in their making wines which can be classified as top quality on a world wide scale.

The Australian winemaker appears to be in much the same position as the Australian artist. He does not have the opportunity to travel often to Europe or America; he sees little of overseas changes and, day by day, mutations of style; he is confined to looking at what, in many cases, are inferior examples of overseas production.

On the other hand, the French winemaker is doing very much the same in his sphere of art as the painter living in Paris. The top French winemakers absorb, almost unconsciously, new ideas from their colleagues, try new techniques, adopt some and abandon many. They look frequently at the top class wines of other districts; talk frequently to other winemen from all over the world; are aware of trends and generally keep abreast of what is happening at the moment in the world of wine.

This does not necessarily make them better winemakers than our winemakers; nor does it mean that European methods of making would suit, unconditionally, our particular climate.

Nonetheless, it can result in our wines being out of fashion on a world market. It can mean that our top wines are so different as to prevent them from contending for the honours in competition with wines from other parts of the world.

Winemakers, no matter how conscious of their ability, should be willing to listen avidly to overseas opinion on our wines; to listen to men who know wine and who travel overseas a great deal. The best substitute for living in Europe for some years is to travel there often.

Admittedly, we have a number of winemakers who read thoroughly around their subject, who often taste the wines

of other countries; who make it their duty to travel often
and to pick up trends and ideas; and, most importantly,
are deep thinkers.

It is the opinions of such winemakers which must be
carefully weighed in the search for the outstanding wines
of Australia.

OPINIONS OF OUR SMALL OWNER/WINEMAKERS
If I were to go to each small winemaker in Australia and
ask him his ideas on what qualities constitute a great
wine, I feel sure that most of the answers would differ
from state to state.

I feel sure also that in any compact, highly integrated
area such as Rutherglen, Swan Valley or the Hunter River
most of the answers would be similar. Each small agricultural community has its *idée fixe* which has been formu-
lated over many years and has been consolidated by
countless conversations over bar counters and at railway
sidings. Once a collection of theories has become area
lore, it is extremely unlikely that it will be changed.

The farmer and the winemaker are of a kind. Over a
century or more the winemaker, his father and his grand-
father have discovered the most competent way of
producing the best from the land they have cultivated.
They are not self-opinionated nor strong in defence of
their methods. Theirs is a philosophy of resignation based
on the knowledge that nature dictates most of what
occurs in the manner in which things grow. If they are to
succeed, they can follow only proven methods of dealing
with the vagaries of nature.

Hence the Hunter Valley man can nod with approval
when he hears the theories of the man from McLaren Vale.
He willingly concedes that modern methods of winemaking
introduced from France may be better than his own and
he is happy to try them. Underneath his acquiescence,
however, he has the knowledge that the character of his
area will always show through and that in the final analysis
varied weather conditions of any year may call for time

Early pickings of grenache grapes entering crusher at Stanley Wine
Co.

Preceding page: Plantings in the Seven Hills district of the Clare
Valley, S.A. Some of the producing vines in this region are over
100 years old.

proved and area proved methods of handling.

Reg Drayton of Pokolbin shows himself typical of the small, close-to-the-earth, winemaker. Beneath the farmer's exterior he emerges as a very shrewd, experienced wineman expressing very clearly the viticultural philosophy of the Hunter winemakers. W. Drayton and Sons are a fraternity in a true sense since all the partners are brothers, cousins, fathers or uncles. They work as a team, each partner with his own particular duties, but all are possessed with a common viticultural and business ideology. Their combined wealth is great enough to ward off the attacks of the English and American raiders in takeovers.

Despite the variations, depicted by Max Lake, between the wines of the different Hunter wineries, there is a character common to all wines of the region which is well illustrated by the products of the Drayton family.

Reg Drayton, winemaker for the partnership, very positively defines *great* Hunter wines. The whites, he says, all tend towards white burgundy style – no matter whether the grapes are picked early or late, what varieties are used or whether the wine is aged in oak or stainless steel.

The reds have their full soft district character modified from year to year because of the troublesome summer rains.

Maturation of both reds and whites is rapid because of the high summer temperatures which in parts of the wineries reach 49°C.

Reg believes in modern methods and readily accepts new concepts of winemaking, always with the proviso that they may prove to be no more effective than the old. Thus his family believe in and employ controlled cold fermentation for both reds and whites. They use stainless steel storage for some of their whites, but are coming to believe that a better flavour is produced from the ancient casks of German oak. They have tried some new American for the reds, but are not risking their entire vintage of reds with this procedure which is possibly unsuitable for Hunter wines.

When nature is kind Reg Drayton produces top quality and typical Hunter wines. He does not claim that they are outstanding wines compared on a world standard, because he would not pretend to know if they were. He is content that his wines are made in a fashion which best suits the area and that as Australian wines they are of great quality.

As a rule, the small winemaker is no judge of quality outside his own district. Even with the wines of his own area his assessment of quality is so localized that it is of little value to a wine buyer from outside the area.

I suppose this could be as true of Burgundy in France as it is of north-east Victoria. Winemakers outside Australia rely on their buying public to learn what are the quality wines of their districts.

Alexis Lichine, who tentatively reclassified in order of merit the great wines of France, relied almost entirely on public assessment. 'Most of the experts consulted', he said, 'were of the opinion that, in assessing the position of the vineyards, price would still be (as it was in 1855), the most reliable indicator; and it was on this basis that (my) classification was prepared.'

Discussions with Owen Redman have convinced me that the small winemaker does not always know the wine quality of his area. Elsewhere I stated that in my opinion Owen Redman has been making the best reds at Coona-warra for five or six years. He has enough gold awards to prove that. This is so, I believe, because of three reasons: he is a first class winemaker; he uses top quality grapes and he is a *small* winemaker.

Related to the fact that he is a good winemaker is his use of new oak, both Nevers (French) and American. Coonawarra reds are improved by a touch of oak flavour just as much as Bordeaux reds. Owen gives just the right amount of ageing to his wine in these new casks. Too much could result in a wine which is far too 'oaky' and a flavour disaster. But will he keep on buying new oak or will his new oak casks become old and seasoned like so many thousands of casks already in South Australian wineries?

Owen Redman does not make his wine from grapes grown on the black soil but only from those grown on the red 'terra rossa', because, so he says, 'wine from the black soil is not one that you would market as a straight Coonawarra. It needs blending with wine from the red soil, or another district'.

This assessment seems too provincial to me. There may be difficulties associated with growing grapes on the Coonawarra black soil but if they are allowed to ripen sufficiently they will make top quality wines.

Owen can be described as a 'natural' winemaker. He judges the state of maturity of the grape by its appearance and his personal tasting of the juice. A small winemaker of his experience and skill does not need to know Baume reading or acid content.

The large companies, with their huge hectares of grapes, however, cannot work with such simple practices. Scientific planning is necessary for them to determine the right time to begin picking. I am convinced that they, too, will make in great quantities, some of the best reds in Australia, from both the Coonawarra red and black soils.

OPINIONS OF OUR WINE JUDGES

If the wine shows of Australia are to have any value in enabling us to establish a classification of the outstandingly high-quality wines in this country, then clearly the system of granting awards must provide results that are consistent in them all.

Wine judges must have a uniform idea of the quality they are seeking. It is quite obvious that at present they do not.

One judge, for example, will have an idea of a 'burgundy' as a full, soft wine, heavy in character with a dark colour. He will reject as 'out of style' a wine light in colour and texture, although it might have roundness, softness, plentiful flavour and perfect balance. Another might assess the second wine as being a perfect 'burgundy' according well in style with the best burgundies of France. Perhaps there should be a school for wine judges.

Judges must have a degree of competence beyond any doubt. The firm of Penfold, with its great team of highly trained winemakers, its highly expensive equipment and its most efficient wineries, must sometimes be aggrieved when it looks through a team of judges that has given scant appreciation to its entries only to find that there are several there who come from remote wineries of no stature, whose reputations as winemakers are not great and whose opportunities of tasting a great number of the high-class wines of the world are limited.

An ideal wine judge possesses many qualities. Certainly he must be intelligent. He must also possess mental balance and a broad outlook on life without prejudice or bias. His mind should be well ordered and he should be able to assess situations quickly. A training in logical thinking such as is provided by tertiary education or experience in an executive capacity is almost as important. Sensitive organs of taste and smell and a good palate memory are essential. He must love wine and drink it constantly in preference to any other beverage. He must have drunk thoughtfully a great deal of wine from all parts of Australia. He should have a great deal of experience of the best of French, Italian and Spanish wines and, as well, a passing knowledge of the other wines of the world.

We would expect, therefore, that wine merchants of the specialist type make the best judges. Scientists from the Wine Research Institute, dedicated restaurateurs, executive type winemakers from large companies who handle wine from several areas and, finally, the businessman who, semi-retired, has adopted wine as his abiding hobby: all are potentially fine show judges.

Our ideal judge will probably be living in a capital city, have many friends with the same interest in wine and food and thus keep in daily touch with the wines of the world.

The greatest mental blockage the wine judge has to overcome in his assessment of wine is the common error of confusing familiarity with quality. This tendency of human nature warps judgement in all fields. Aligning this human and only too common trait with our assessment of wine, I often feel tempted to halt the unadulterated praise I sometimes hear about certain district wines of Australia by asking the question, 'Aren't you overpraising these wines because you have become too familiar with their taste?'

In self condemnation I know that I make exactly the same error. As soon as I smell a Coonawarra red I am pre-disposed to give it top marks for quality even before I have tasted it. Is this because since early youth I have identified top quality with Bordeaux, and Coonawarra reminds me of Bordeaux?

Without prejudice (I hope) I feel that much the same thing happens with our admirers of Hunter Valley reds. Max Lake in his book *Hunter Winemakers* leaves one with the impression that there is no red wine in the world that can quite compare with a Hunter. The same tendency seems to have captivated so many of our top wine men that I wonder if we have not developed a 'Hunter Valley' palate. I can remember how deeply impressed I have been with the quality and flavour of the Mt Pleasant and Lindeman reds of the late thirties and of all the forties. Even today, oxidised and tired as most of them are, the mere taste of one of them produces a paean of praise in my head and I try to communicate my feelings of wonderment that such beauty of bouquet and flavour has survived so long.

Yet am I being only nostalgic, sentimental, lovingly reminiscent of a familiar thing? Has the fact that our best early efforts in wine making came from this great valley given us a tradition which is so deeply ingrained in our thinking that we cannot eradicate for a moment our penchant for these soft red wines? Is it so strong that we influence our tyros to wine, our overseas guests and our new migrants into thinking the same way?

In a more attenuated fashion Australian wine drinkers as a whole have an 'Australian orientated' palate for their reds. Most of us would prefer the rich, flavorous wines of

McLaren Vale and Angaston to the thin reds of Southern Burgundy or to the astringent Chianti. We should remember that this attitude can never be a criterion of quality. It is simply a reflection of our reaction to the taste of something with which we are well acquainted; the Australian preference for fresh rather than sour cream which continentals relish so much; our choice of aerated ice cold beer on a wintry day in preference to the flat warm beer of the English public house.

How often do we hear the plaintiff cry of our older wine men, 'why can't we get the great heavy reds from Rutherglen anymore?'—you could almost stand a spoon in them. Let us be frank with ourselves. Would this kind of wine be accepted in the world of today? The answer is 'no!'

Yet we cannot write off our national preference for Hunter Valley reds as being entirely due to familiarity. They do in many cases have quality characteristics which place them in a line-up of the best wines of Australia and in some special cases, the best wines of the world.

Climatically one would not be inclined to think it probable. Yet there are climatic variations from the norm in all parts of Australia. Some areas of the Hunter Valley, Clare and parts of the Barossa Ranges are typical examples.

Everyone who has taken any interest in wine – other than the person who thinks of wine as a pleasant drink to go with a meal and nothing more – knows how wine judging works in Australia. It takes place yearly in the cities of Melbourne, Adelaide, Sydney and Brisbane. Fundamentally, it is based on picking the best wines in certain styles: light dry red style, 'hock' class, 'white burgundy' class, etc. Gold medal awards are made to winners in every particular class. Two gold medals may be awarded if the first two wines are inseparable. Special awards are given to the company which has gained the greatest number of gold, silver and bronze medals. There are special trophies for a number of other special successes, for example, 'the most successful exhibitor in all light table wine classes' or 'the best pale fino sherry'.

Wine shows provide a lot of excitement to all those who partake in them and to those who win awards. They are also big business. For months after awards are announced, full page advertisements appear in the papers announcing the award winners, medals and trophies.

Wine shows serve one very great purpose; they provide competition and therefore stimulate winemakers to aim for perfection. In this way the more wine shows there are the better it is for the industry. Experienced judges can point out faults in wines and show the erring winemaker in which direction he should be headed. The appearance of a collection of competitive wines in one place enables the various winemakers to compare, question and learn.

OPINIONS OF OUR LEADING AMATEURS

Apart from the winemakers themselves and the results of the wine shows, where are we to look to reach judgement on the outstanding wines of Australia? The answer surely must lie in asking the men and women in Australia who have made reputations for themselves as people who know good wine. We can find them in many cities of Australia. As I have spent most of my life in Melbourne, I feel that in this city, at least, I am qualified to select a band of wine men whose opinions are worth hearing.

The best judges of wine in Australia collect around the monthly table of the Viticultural Society of Victoria. This is a semi-professional society but each member, and often each guest, whether professional or amateur, is so highly endowed with a wealth of wine knowledge and has such balanced judgement that I should be hard put to find one whose opinion on any particular wine I would not gladly accept as true. Membership of this society is limited to fifty. Before a member is elected he must have had many years of experience in wine and must have, besides more personal qualities, some reputation as a wine man. Some have been members for almost half a century. On regarding these men, I realise why their reputations loom large upon the wine scene.

Doyen of Melbourne wine men, David Sutherland Smith, is a man with a fantastic memory for wines. In spite of a penchant for the local product in preference to the French, he is a very great guide to what is the best in wine. Then there is Douglas Seabrook who in my judgement is one of the best wine show judges in Australia. He has the ability accurately to limn in detail a great Australian wine and to compare it in detail with a great wine of France. Ron Emerson, experienced and dedicated, devotes a life to the appreciation of wine and his judgement is accurate and true. Simon Borten, whose tremendous experience of top-quality French wine is possibly the greatest of all, uses it skilfully to weigh up the merits of every Australian wine. Geoffrey Donaldson, famed in business circles, adds to his other great abilities that of being able to rightly assess the best wines of the country. Douglas Crittenden, wine merchant and connoisseur, never errs when assessing the quality of a great wine. Bruce Coulter, Gordon Blackburn, John Butler, John Collie, Bill Davies, Frank Devine, Roy Duncan, Bruce Hallows, Clifford Heard, Stan Keon and Ian Sutherland Smith rarely fail to astonish me with the breadth and depth of their wine knowledge and their true assessment of every wine placed before them.

There are others, too, in this city of excellent wine, like accountant Ken Keown; restaurateurs Ian Hickinbotham and Herman Schneider; and solicitor Reg Egan, whose opinions on wine are worth seeking. Among the women, Joyce Garretty and Lorraine Walker amaze me.

If the names of famed Melbourne wine men are omitted in this short summary, it is only because there are so many hundreds in Melbourne.

Nevertheless, it is these men and women such as those whose voices from across the country have helped me, over the years, to build up a very clear impression of what are the great and outstanding wines of Australia. They have done more in this respect than the winemakers and the wine shows. The frank, unbiased opinions of these experienced men and women, about wines presented to them anonymously in unmarked glasses, have enabled me to create a category of first class Australian vineyards.

MY PERSONAL OPINIONS

The thousands of bottles of red wine which I have drunk at least give me the right to express an opinion on the subject, though it may not be entirely in accord with that of my confrères in the wine game.

Laboriously, I have endeavoured to draw a correspondence between climate and quality. Climate includes the whole synthesis of hours of sunshine, summation of heat received from the sun, annual rainfall, hail, frost, cloud and mist. It is not entirely related to degrees of latitude, nor altitude nor proximity to the sea, nor to wind patterns, nor again to the time of the year when top temperatures are prevalent.

Related to quality wine grapes, climate is closely connected to such local factors as hills and valleys, northern and southern slopes, the path of thunderstorms, the swirl pattern of air around clumps of trees or mounds which deters the formation of frosts, cloud formation and the period in which rain begins to fall in the autumn.

All these things, need a great deal of elaboration and there is no space for that in this book.

But my assessment of the most likely areas to produce the top quality wines of Australia in the next hundred years has not been influenced just by the consumption of the contents of those thousands of bottles I mentioned earlier, but by years of study and the opinion of men I respect.

Many Australian areas which I have not included in the classification do in fact produce wonderful red wines which are full of flavour, attractive colour and compare well with highly regarded wines from France, Italy, Spain, Portugal and California; but they cannot qualify in competition with the *top quality* wines of Bordeaux, Burgundy, Piedmont and Napa Valley.

There is the crux of the matter. No matter what our personal opinion of some odd wine coming from an area without much reputation, it is not of much consequence when we relate it to the top wines of the world.

At this stage of Australian wine development, we should be able to produce a list of wine districts which consistently produce our best wines.

The world's experts know that expertise. and modern equipment can sometimes result in extremely good wines coming from unlikely areas. This same expertise and modern equipment should be able to produce even greater wines from our classic areas.

The developing areas included in the 'classic' classification have not yet justified themselves. I am basing my hopes on a high degree of probability. Yarra Valley and Geelong scarcely exist as wine areas. I can only hope that some of the prosperous investment companies who have been so lavish in the Hunter Valley will let a few crumbs fall around these promising areas.

Summarily, therefore, despite my calling upon other authoritative sources, the basis of the classification is my personal opinion.

OVERSEAS OPINIONS
Following my discussions in *The Age* some years ago regarding quality wines in Australia, it was interesting to receive in the mail an extract from *The San Francisco Examiner* of the 17th February, 1971, entitled 'Living wine – Australia's Exotics'. Too infrequently do we hear an unprejudiced opinion of Australia's wine by wine experts from overseas countries. This article was obviously written by an authoritative wine writer quite unconsciously assessing the quality of Australian wines obtainable in the U.S.A. From the tone of the article I would say that he knew his subject well and that the basis of his comparison was Californian wine. He neither praises nor condemns the Australian product but much of what he says is in line with what I have been writing for years. It would be worthwhile to take notice of his gentle criticism.

He writes, 'the outstanding single fact is that the Australians – winemakers and public alike – favour the taste of age more than we do'. And continues, 'age shows up more strongly in the reds along with plenty of tannin . . . the Aussies enjoy tannins in amounts that would tan a sheep's hide in ten days flat'. It is obvious again that the writer does not condemn age in a wine if it is a wine that is intended for long ageing. I do not doubt that if he had tasted (which he apparently has not) a 1959 Coonawarra he would not have considered it any more unusually aged than a Chateau Latour of the same year; but he is obviously surprised that medium quality reds from Australia show signs of age and the implication is that they are not worth ageing. They should be drunk young. Again he writes, 'curiously, the majority of reds showed distinct tinges of brown. Tannin inhibits the browning of red wines for years on end. So, as the evening wore on the succession of ambered wines made it clear that this oxidation is not just tolerated, but rather is actively sought'. We cannot blame the writer for thinking that Australians like their wine oxidised because all their reds begin to show a distinct brownish tinge long before they ought, thus giving the appearance of greater age than their years would warrant. If we are to be criticised in America because our red wines show signs of oxidation then perhaps our winemakers had better have a reassessment of one or two aspects of their winemaking methods. If it were possible, I would deny the fact that comparatively young wines show too much browning but unfortunately it is true in too many cases. Unfortunately, also, many of these wines are being kept by would-be connoisseurs in the vain hope that they will improve further.

The Wine Research Institute is justifiably concerned with the fact that many Australian dry reds do in fact show signs of oxidation even after twelve months. The beautiful bright red colour that we should see is just not there. Very often a twelve months' old wine has the appearance of one six or seven years' old. The Institute has published at least one paper on the cause of this browning and I can only wish that every Australian winemaker would obtain a copy of it.

The complaint about tannin is justifiable. I am glad that a wine expert from another country has pointed out the errors of our ways in trying to extract from an oaken cask a chemical which does very little to enhance the flavour of wine. As I have said the American article was not really critical. On the contrary the tone was such as to encourage Americans to try Australian wines for themselves, the implication being that they were different from the American product but good.

However, it does point out the uselessness of seeking opinions on our wines from overseas sources. We are, of course, selling more and more wine in other countries but it is of a type which would not lead foreign experts to classify our wines as top quality. That is the problem. Overseas experts do not see our top quality wines unless they come to Australia.

3 Do Outstanding Wines come only from Outstanding Wine Areas?

It is significant that France does not classify wine areas overtly. She certainly classifies vineyards within an area but is most cautious about grading one area above another. However the mere selection of an area by the Institut National des Appellations d'Origine *ipso facto* classifies it above areas which have not been selected. One could say the same about areas in Italy which have been authorized by the government to use the system of Denominazione di Origine Controllata.

Any country which wishes to introduce a system of the guarantee of quality of their wines obviously must look to France, Italy and Germany for guidance. It would be difficult to improve on their control laws except as they relate to the problems of our own country. They are basically the same. Government appointed bodies lay down in general the specified area of production for the controlled district, the types of vines that may be grown, the minimum alcoholic content, the viticultural practices, the permissible maximum harvest of a specified area and the vinicultural practices.

If the Australian Government were to make similar laws for the Australian wine industry it would be faced with a great number of difficulties as regards permitted grape varieties. We have not as yet a crystallised formula which automatically dictates what are the best wine varieties for any particular area. The older countries have.

The immediate task is to decide which areas in Australia produce outstanding wines. I do not intend to grade one area as against another nor even to classify the wineries within an area. It will be at least a century before anything like that can be done.

There is always a temptation to believe that matters are improving, that the situation is getting better. It is not true, particularly, as regards wine areas. If the Hunter Valley had a remarkable year for red wines only once on an average every six years in the first half of this century, it will have a remarkable year only once every six years for the next half of this century and for the century after, and the century after that. If the Murray Valley produced only mediocre red wines in the fifties, it will keep on producing mediocre wines for as long as it matters to us.

We are apt to be carried away by new techniques, new grape varieties, enthusiastic and capable winemakers, but, in the end, it is all to no avail. It is nature which determines all. Man can only go along with nature and produce the best he can within its limitations.

The French have the Midi. The Italians have Campania. Spain has Catalonia; Portugal Lagoa; all of which goes to demonstrate that the largest wine producing countries in the world have huge tracts of vineyards planted for the sole purpose of supplying enormous quantities of low price, average quality wine to the indigenous masses. Certainly, these countries have their Bordeaux, their Piedmont, their Rioja and their Oporto to lend prestige to their viticulture; But these areas are not for the constant, lower income every day drinker.

One might think sometimes from the writing of our wine enthusiasts that we have no great bulk wine areas, that every wine district was either a Bordeaux or a Burgundy. But I believe we do indeed have our Midi, our mass production wine areas which rarely produce top quality wines but which continually bring forward enormous quantities of tolerable wine which is best sold in flagons or similar bulk forms.

The contentious point is whether winemakers in these areas also make first class wines worthy of affording competition to great Hunters, Coonawarras or Great Westerns. I think they do not, but there will be many who disagree. It is possible that the rare and occasional gem, from a combination of unusual circumstances, will appear just as one brilliant, pure, clear diamond will be found sometimes in acres of garnets.

The flagon areas of Australia must be the districts along the Murray River from Mildura in Victoria to Waikerie in South Australia; the Murrumbidgee Irrigation Area of New South Wales and the Swan Valley of Western Australia. If we take them simply as flagon wines there can be no controversy about the excellence of the wines from these areas.

It seems to have been an economic principle of Australian winemaking that since the turn of the century only wine of a fairly high standard was to be made. Because the competition from beer and spirits was, and is, so intense, land that could produce only low class wines was far more profitably utilized in other directions, such as for general farming or sheep growing. The flagon wine drinker is therefore consuming a far better wine than his counterpart in France, Italy, Spain and Portugal.

The great national flagon marketers, Wynn's, McWilliam's and Penfolds obtain their wine for the purpose from the Riverina (or Murrumbidgee) area. These are beautiful reds, whites and rosés. McWilliam's have probably collected more medals from wines made in the Riverina district than most firms have from any other region. That does not, in my book, make them classic wines but it certainly serves to indicate that flagon wines from this area are remarkably good value.

The great co-operatives dominate the Murray River scene and, as their combined total must be over half the wine produced in Australia, and they have very little market for wine under their own labels, there is a certainty that a great percentage of wines sold in flagons, one gallon, five gallon and ten gallon containers comes from them. Some will be marketed by large national companies and a great deal will be sold by groups of retailers under a group label or even by a single retailer under his particular mark.

Whatever the case, they are very superior wines.

Nonetheless, not only district, but care and attention to making, grape variety, accidents of year, cask and control, all determine the relative qualities of wine. That is why the price of flagon table wines vary to such an extent.

One of the most interesting recent investigations by the Australian Wine Research Institute dealt with the effect of climate and soil on the flavour and quality of wine. The Institute employed a tasting panel selected from its own staff and over several years conducted masked tastings of wines from Barossa Valley, Eden Valley and Berri in the Murray Valley. The final analysis showed that, although there was always a difference of quality detectable between the white wines of the dry and the irrigation areas, there was no significant difference between those of the Barossa and Eden Valleys in spite of their difference in climate and soil.

This study must cause wine men to evaluate more carefully the wines of the Murray Valley. The intensive, prolonged and highly organized tastings of recognized wine authorities over a narrow range of wines for a period of years can be regarded only as the acme of perfection in assessing wine quality. The Institute concluded that 'Wines made from irrigated vineyards in the warm River Murray viticultural region, contained similar amounts of tartaric and malic acids, but were higher in pH, than wines made from the same grape varieties in the cooler non-irrigated Barossa Valley. *Wines from irrigated grapes were generally of somewhat lower quality* than those made from grapes of the same variety grown without irrigation in a cooler area.' ('Influence of grape variety, climate and soil on grape composition and on the composition and quality of table wines' by B. C. Rankine, J. C. M. Fornachon, E. W. Boehm and K. M. Cellier. *Australian Wine Research Pamphlet No. 84*, 1971).

Of course, I cannot use this paper as an argument that quality wines come only from quality areas but it does help build up the picture.

cannot be sure. Perhaps a Lindeman's Hunter Valley Burgundy is a greater wine; or the laurel wreath might go to Redman's Coonawarra.

Before we go far in classifying Australian wines it is important to decide what areas are worth classifying. The French have been very slow about grading wines in not-so-famous areas in Medoc such as Pomerol and this small region has had to fight hard for official recognition despite its unofficially recognized excellence. Côtes de Bourg, Côtes de Blaye and St Emilion-Lussac are not likely to be classified officially at all even though they produce beautiful Bordeaux wines. The well known areas of other regions of France such as the Rhone Valley, Provence and the Loire Valley are not yet considered by French Authorities as worthy of grading according to merit or reputation. This is despite the fact that Professor George Saintsburg in his *Notes from a Cellar Book* debated whether an 1864 Hermitage (Rhone Valley) or an 1858 Romanée Conti was the greatest vintage he had known, and the famous Alphonse Daudet called Chateauneuf-du-Pape (again Rhone Valley) the 'King of Wines, Wine of Kings'.

If the French are so reluctant about setting up lists in order of quality of their famous districts, how much more careful should we be in Australia where we have no government-appointed committee on the naming of wines nor even strong traditions which would make classifications acceptable.

Where should we begin? Certainly we should include the Hunter Valley at least in the older region around Pokolbin. Should we take in the region known as the Riverina or Murrumbidgee Irrigation Area? Would we be wise to include north-east Victoria? Coonawarra is beyond doubt, but what of Langhorne Creek?

Brave is the man who endeavours to decide that certain wine areas should be selected and others neglected. Yet if we are to begin, such a division must be made. Someone must make a start; after all what has he got to lose but all his friends in the wine trade?

Classification of Vineyards within an area

I have decided that it is wise not to grade vineyards within an area according to a supposed quality rating. It was difficult enough for the burghers of the Medoc in 1755 to classify sixty-three chateaux in order of excellence; but at least they had the auction system, or a kind of offer system as a basis. If wine merchants were prepared to offer a hundred times as much for a cask of Chateau Latour as for one of Chateau Cantemerle it is obvious that the former is to be placed near the top of the list and the latter near the bottom.

We have nothing like that to guide us in Australia. It would be sheer folly to endeavour to place a grading on any vineyard in Australia.

I believe it would be impossible to give a classification of vineyards within an area in this book.

IT IS THE VINEYARD THAT MATTERS

You will notice that, where possible, I take note of the vineyard not of the proprietor. Thus at Coonawarra, I refer to Redbank (not Redman's), to Laira (not Brand's); at Great Western it is Concongella (not Thomson's).

Naturally with the vineyards of the large companies the company name is important and in most cases they have not named their vineyards. In consequence, I refer to Wynn's Coonawarra (rather than Coonawarra Estate) and to Mildara Coonawarra. Both these companies have several vineyards at Coonawarra and it is conceivable that in the future they will label their special wines with the name of the particular vineyard where the grapes were grown.

It is a matter of identification. Chances are that Owen Redman or his heirs will sell out one day or that Thomson's will be taken over by a larger company. If a classification is to have any value then one must be reasonably sure that the name under which a vineyard is entered in the classification will endure for centuries.

It would be nice and tidy, of course, if we could have a system like the French where the wineries in Bordeaux are called chateaux and in Burgundy carry names that go back into history such as Clos de Vougeot or Romanée Conti. The name of the proprietor is incidental. Indeed it is extremely unlikely that even connoisseurs of French wines could tell you the names of more than one or two proprietors although they may be able to reel off hundreds of vineyard names.

That does not mean that the proprietor is not important. The reputation of even the great chateaux of the Medoc have gone up and down like a bug on a vine with changes of proprietors, some of whom have been enthusiastic and some who used the chateau like a country estate.

In a new country such as Australia we have few traditional vineyard names. Our wine writers have laid great stress on the importance of the individual winemakers who, very often, are proprietors. Little attention has been given to the fact that, no matter who owns the vineyard, once it has built up a reputation for producing outstanding wines, that reputation will cling to it.

It is well to call to mind that, in Australia, the vineyard and the winery are rarely juxta-positioned. To quote from my *Australian Wine: The Complete Guide:*

'It would probably be misleading merely to list wineries. The use of the word "winery" as opposed to "vineyard" is desirable. For the purpose of categorizing districts, the place where the grape is grown is the important thing. In most instances, the vinegrower is a distinct identity from the winemaker. Australian practice generally is to buy grapes from a man who has no interest in them once they go to the winery. The exception is the high quality vineyard and winery where it is essential to operate growing and making as one unified whole. Even this winery will supplement its supplies by purchasing grapes from one or two smaller growers who are independent of the winery'.

Obviously, this present book is dealing almost entirely with wineries of the latter type. Even so, this does not mean that we can assume that every high quality winery is processing grapes only from its immediate district.

We can take Buring's as a good example. There can be no question that their winery at Tanunda in the Barossa Valley puts out some of the greatest white wines in the world. Very few of the grapes from which these wines are made come from the Barossa Valley. Many of them are grown at Clare and in the Barossa Ranges which I categorize as entirely different districts to the Barossa Valley.

Buring's are very careful to describe on their labels what is exactly the truth regarding the areas where the grapes are grown.

If we are to follow the French system, therefore, we would have to pinpoint the very plot of land where the grapes are grown to institute a classification within every area.

Bob Elliott in the Hunter has a winery at **Oakvale** where he also grows grapes. He has a vineyard called **Tallawanta,** and vineyards at **Belford** and **Fordwich**. Each wine made from grapes grown at these vineyards several miles apart is quite different from the others. Most wine men think that Belford whites are the best. Elliott markets most of his wines under the Oakvale label but special binnings give the name of the vineyards.

This is intelligent labelling. It is the vineyard that matters when it comes to classifying wines.

This practice of one winery making and marketing wines from various vineyards is seen in France. Baron Philippe de Rothschild owns and makes the wine of both Chateau Mouton Rothschild and Chateau Mouton-du-Baron Philippe. The two vineyards are adjoining but the wines are made separately. Chateau Mouton Rothschild ranks as a premier cru (first growth) but Chateau Philippe is classified as a Cinquieme Cru (fifth growth).

In Burgundy there are hundreds of small vineyards which make their wines and send them to shippers who bottle them and market them, usually under the parish name. In many cases the shipper is also the proprietor of several vineyards. He may make the wine at his winery, bottle it and label it with the name of the vineyard where the grapes were grown. As Alexis Lichine says, the Burgundians have a saying, 'Respectez les crus'. He says this means, 'learn the name of the best growths or vineyards, and pay no attention to any other names'.

It is the vineyard that matters. Wineries may draw their grape supplies from a number of vineyards, even from within the same area. A classification of vineyards according to quality is impossible unless the maker identifies on his label the exact vineyard from whence came the grapes.

It would add nothing to our wine knowledge simply to classify wineries. In some wild fantasy we could imagine a dozen wineries setting up on the outskirts of Sydney, all drawing their supplies of grapes from various districts and producing the best wine in Australia. This is virtually what is happening in the Barossa now. Wineries are drawing grape supplies from all over South Australia and making superb wines. Any attempt at classification would simply be a classification of wine making techniques, individual viticultural skills and management.

We do know, mostly because of the integrity of the makers, where the grapes that make the best wines are grown. In many cases we know the precise vineyards where they were grown. We have enough evidence to select the areas which are producing or are likely to produce the best wines of our country.

If wine continues to become more and more popular, it may be economical one day to introduce an 'appellation contrôllée' system. Then we should, after another hundred years or so, be able to classify according to their worth, the best vineyards of Australia. Until then, it will at least be of some value to know that Bendigo, for example, is likely to produce a great dry red wine and that the vineyard producing at present is owned by Stuart Anderson; or that the Hunter Valley is a top ranking wine area and that the top wines come from Lindeman's, McWilliam's, Penfold's, Rothbury, Max Lake and a few others.

At this stage of our development, do we want to know more?

BLENDED WINES

Obviously wines blended from various areas cannot be included in a classification of areas. One can hardly imagine the French blending a wine from Burgundy with one from Bordeaux and I have never felt that there has been a good enough reason to justify blending Hunters with Coonawarras.

Admittedly there have been some excellent wines produced by such blending. **Mildara Bin 21 Cabernet-Shiraz** and subsequent binnings are fine examples. Yet, to my mind, they add very little to our gamut of top wines. Dedicated wine men prefer their wines to come from one area only. There is a satisfaction in knowing that a certain vineyard and that alone was responsible for a great wine.

Grange Hermitage is undoubtedly the label which identifies a run of the greatest red wines Australia has produced after the war. Only Penfold's records would reveal what were the constituents of this wine in the different years. It is quite possible that it is blended from different areas. Are we then to exclude our greatest wine from a classification of Australian wines? I can see no way out. At various times Penfold's winemakers have said that Grange Hermitage was made from grapes grown at the Grange vineyard at Magill. At other times it has been hinted that the Kalimna vineyards may have been involved. The Grange vineyard has been sold for property development. If Kalimna vineyards were to be used as the only source of Grange, we would have no difficulty because Kalimna certainly qualifies as a very great vineyard.

Would Penfold's place the word 'Kalimna' on the Grange label? Most of the wine giants dislike changing an accepted label and the decision would have to be made by a future board of directors.

NEW AREAS AND NEW VINEYARDS

Obviously a classification can never be complete in a developing community. No sooner is it decided to include all the vineyards in an area than another one has been set up. Is it to be included or left out?

The question is not answered easily. In France it would be easy indeed. Should an enterprising land owner in the Medoc decide to establish a new vineyard in the area, he would learn all about the rules that had to be followed in order to receive the 'appellation contrôlée' accolade for his vineyard. He would plant the varieties of grapes laid down, neither more or less to the hectare than required; cultivate his soil according to directions and abide by all the directions of the local bureau of the Institut National des Appellations d'Origine. Without much difficulty he would be entitled to call his wine 'Medoc'.

In Australia, a man of a similar enterprising nature might decide to set up a vineyard in the Pokolbin area. Without any restrictions from any controlling board, he could plant, let us say, grenache grapes at three times the number to the hectare as all of his neighbours. He could adopt a wild system of overhead trellising, cultivate his land in a most unorthodox manner and ultimately produce the most dreadful kind of red wine. Yet he would still be entitled to label his wine 'Pokolbin'. Do we exclude him from our list of vineyards in our classified area? Frankly, I would.

Following that decision as a general guide, I have included all vineyards which have not yet proved themselves as being up to the standard of existing and proved vineyards only if they conform to the general practices of viticulture as practised in the area. If, at some future date, vineyard proprietors who do not conform to established patterns can prove that their unorthodox methods are successful and they are taking first class wines off their vineyards, then they can be included in the classification.

The position is far more difficult when it comes to entirely new areas. I have included in the classification Geelong, Yarra Valley, Bendigo and a few other areas because the position of the vineyards and the opinions of experts give me sufficient encouragement to include them. Wines so far produced and (in some cases) the reputation of the areas from former times warrant their inclusion.

5 South Australia

The Wines of Clare/Watervale

This is the area situated in the northern Mt Lofty Range around the two towns of Clare and Watervale. The high altitude of Clare compensates for its latitude of 34 degrees which takes it out of the 'cold climate' latitudes of Coonawarra, Drumborg and Great Western. It is, in fact, about the same latitude as the Hunter Valley and, whereas this latter area produces high-quality wines because of its cloud cover in summer and the many hills and slopes which protect the vines from a day-long sun, Clare has a lower mean summer temperature than the Hunter because of its height. Most of the vineyards of Clare are at about 395 metres. Leasingham at Watervale is closer to 425 metres, which brings it nearer to the height of Pewsey Vale and the Steingarten Vineyard of Gramp's in the Barossa Ranges.

These higher areas obviously provide the conditions necessary for quality – slow ripening curves, retention of high acidity in the grapes up to time of full ripeness and harvest time later in the season when the heat of summer has passed.

Climatically, therefore, Clare is more related to Coonawarra than the Hunter. Hunter reds and whites are full, soft wines with plenty of flavour. Their quality is derived from the lesser sun hours experienced as compared with, say, Griffith, which is of a higher latitude. Clare reds and whites are highly acid, firm wines. The number of sun hours experienced over Clare is the same as those of the Barossa and the nearby Murray River areas, but the harsh effect of this factor is negated by the hilly terrain. In the Clare district a vineyard situated on a steep slope facing the east will produce infinitely better wines than one on flat ground and exposed to the sun's rays the whole day through.

Hence vines in the area yield wines of vastly different character and quality to those made from grapes grown on the flats of the Barossa Valley. Some of the rhine riesling grapes grown at Clare and Watervale produce the best riesling-style wines in Australia.

Soil is important in winemaking, not so much from the flavour and quality angle, but because well-moistened, friable soil produces healthy vines which in turn produce healthy grapes in optimum quantities on those particular vines. Many sections of Clare have excellent vineyard soils consisting of red clay loam over limestone. Rainfall is sufficient, being an average of 622·30 mm per year. In the higher areas it is 660·4 mm. Rain occurs mainly in the winter with ample falls occurring in the spring when it is needed most. Like all other vine bearing soils, supplementary watering is necessary in Australia to nurse the vines through the first hard year. Ideally supplementary watering should be available in dry periods for all vines. So far, Clare has not enjoyed this luxury.

Clare is not a large viticultural area. At present there are approximately 1619 hectares planted out with vines and about seven or eight thousand tonnes are cropped at vintage. New plantings are being made every year, both by established companies and by entirely new interests consisting of consortiums or syndicates of business men who realize its potential.

In the past three or four years, whites have received more publicity than the reds, with the Stanley Wine Company gaining dozens of gold and silver medals for its rhine riesling wines. Yet the reds, too, are truly remarkable. In a good year a well made red has a pure crimson colour with great density. This colour remains much the same for many years with little change. The bouquet is clean and rich. The flavour is tremendous – rich and full but with no suggestion of cloying. They are unique reds bearing no resemblance to wine made elsewhere. With improved techniques in handling new oak they will be outstanding. Unfortunately they will be in short supply for a long time.

The present wineries in the area are those of Stanley, Birks, Quelltaler, Clarevale Co-operative, Sevenhill Jesuit Community and Chateau Clare.

A great deal of the material grown in the Clare region in past years has been taken to Barossa Valley wineries where it has been merged with high-quality wines from other areas such as the Barossa Ranges. The wines so produced have appeared under the maker's name.

Leo Buring Pty Ltd is responsible for first-class wines, largely produced from grapes grown in the Clare district. Its holding company, **Lindeman's**, has been an enormous buyer of Clare wines for many years. Lindeman's market them 'straight' under its own name with a description on the label telling where the wine comes from or as part of blends.

Improved marketing methods by Clare companies will probably eliminate the bulk sale of wine to companies outside the area. **Stanley Wine Company**, for example, has merged its interests with H. J. Heinz Ltd. This huge company has already begun to employ its vast marketing machine to sell Stanley Wines to licensed grocers and supermarkets. I have no doubt that they will very quickly sell the entire yearly produce of this winery.

Quelltaler Wines Ltd is one of the Vigneron Distillers and Vintners Ltd companies; Nathan & Wyeth of Melbourne is also associated with them. Quelltaler is producing some magnificent white wines and the selling organization of this well established wine and spirit firm should have no difficulty in selling the winery's entire yearly output.

Clarevale Co-operative Winery is now concentrating on the quality market rather than making a large range of commercially acceptable fortified and non-fortified wines. Perhaps it will continue to sell in bulk to other wine companies and to wine merchants.

Sevenhill is geared almost exclusively to making altar wine for the Catholic Church, and it is not likely that this practice will change.

At **Clare** vineyards at Armagh just out of Clare are the personal property of J. B. Barry and his wife. Jim Barry is interested in making first quality table wines typical of the district. He is also associated with **Chateau Clare** which is owned by a syndicate which has vineyards and a winery at Auburn a few miles south of Clare.

Of course, every Clare wine will not be a first-class vintage, but almost all wines will be above average quality and many of them will be first-class wines. I have no hesitation in classifying the Clare district as 'outstanding'.

The Barossa Valley and Surrounding Areas

There are certain classical areas in Australia which produce *outstanding* wines, but from time to time many regions other than these produce *great* wines.

The reasons for this are simple. Firstly no man can lay claim to infallibility (even though in the field of outstanding wines I would like to possess this convenient ecclesiastical quality). It is likely, therefore, that some areas which I have not regarded as classical, produce wines possessing virtues which have been hidden from my eyes (or my taste buds).

We are also presented with the difficulty of winemakers who, given a modicum of potentially successful material, can make, by pure technique, a wine which emulates, and is taken to be, a classic. I must add, as a rider, that such monumental ability seems to be confined to the making of red wine and stems almost entirely from the winemaker's genius in handling oak storage.

In the Barossa Valley **Gramp's** have produced many classical whites for many years from material grown on the flats and lower slopes of the valley. **Penfold's** have marketed wonders under their 'Special Bin' labels, either from straight Barossa (Kalimna Vineyard) or from blends of Barossa and Adelaide Hills material. **Bin 707** and **389** are greatly sought after and probably under-priced but I often wonder whether it is the material used or the wizardry of the Penfold's Magill and Auldana winemakers that is the essence of their success. **Kaiser Stuhl** bottled a magnificent red under the title of **P7214 Shiraz 1964**, but again, without query, the skilful use of oak was the keynote of the operation.

Gramp's have employed a variation of their white wine fermentation technique to make occasional outstanding red under the name of **Barossa Cabernet** or **'Selected Wine' Hermitage.**

The temptation to suggest that the winemaker is the successful ingredient in a quality wine must be resisted. The reputation of an area can rest only on the quality of its grapes.

All the great Barossa rieslings of Gramp's since 1953 have been made from grapes grown on the foothills bordering the Valley. John Vickery of Burings; Jim Irvine, formerly of Hardy's and now of Glen View and Wolf Blass, formerly of Tolley Scott and Tolley and now on his own, have demonstrated that great white wines can be made from Barossa Valley material. Kaiser Stuhl, Penfold's, Gramp's, Salter's and Yalumba have, from time to time, produced classic reds from Barossa Valley grapes.

What is significant is that the great wines are appearing more frequently in recent years.

Although no wine authority has ever written off the Barossa Valley as a top quality area, I cannot remember any one of them giving it a special accolade as a constant producer of world class table wines. Winemakers themselves have sung its praises but winemakers at times are apt to sound like football team coaches. The more often top quality Barossa wine turns up at the tables of wine connoisseurs, the greater is its chance of being recognized as a quality table wine area.

The history of the Barossa has largely been one of fortified wine. Until a few years ago grape varieties which were grown were selected for their particular ability to be converted economically into good ports, muscats, dry sherries, sweet sherries and madeiras.

The conversion of tastes in the fifties and sixties resulted in a revolution in the grape fields; but, whereas a wine drinker can change from being a sweet sherry toper to a claret lover in a matter of months, it takes many years to convert a vineyard to cope with his conversion.

Seppelt's, masters of the Barossa Valley, ten or twelve years ago found that they were lumbered with hundreds of acres of vines they would have preferred not to have. All Seppelt's hands were put to the wheel and it slowly turned. Unprofitable poor bearing vines were rooted out. In some cases they were not replanted. Some soils were considered not really suited to growing grapes. The Seppelt machine meantime, however, had been busy planting in more economic and classic areas and making great wines; yet the Barossa Valley reds and whites seem invariably to have been blended in with wines made from grapes grown by them in other districts. Sooner or later we must see some top quality straight Barossa Valley table wines produced by this superbly efficient company.

The number of smaller makers in the Valley who are bringing forth minor masterpieces is almost startling.

I first saw **Penfold's** winery at Nuriootpa, right in the centre of the Barossa Valley, in 1953. At that time it was under the management of a forceful character named Scholtz who had been there almost from the time Leslie Penfold Hyland built the place in 1902. Today, Penfold's Nuriootpa is a mighty place. To give you some idea of its size, it is sufficient to say that its total capacity is between 20,457 and 22,730 kilolitres. It has 106 fermenters in its 'big' cellar and 50 outside.

Of course, the establishment has actually grown almost imperceptibly over the years. The most recent addition is an iron building adjacent to the old one and used simply for the purpose of crushing white grapes. Inside there is a magnificent set-up of four Mac pre-drainers set over fluted crushers and underground tanks. The juice is pumped to the next door winery for fermentation and the remaining must, consisting largely of skins, pulp and seeds, is transported by must pump to a three phase Mac Press.

By and large the Nuriootpa plant is used only for making fortified wines and brandy.

Over recent years there has been a growing similarity of style between the various table wines of Australia, irrespective of where they are made. The more thoughtful observers have attributed this similarity to the increasingly efficient techniques of viticulture and winemaking being adopted in all areas of Australia. Due to a combination of these three factors, it is becoming more and more difficult to decide whether a wine has come from one of the old classical areas such as Coonawarra or Pokolbin or from areas once not so highly regarded such as the Barossa or Griffith.

Fitting nicely into this pattern of increasing perfection is the vineyard and winery known as **Saltram**. Saltram's are in the Barossa Valley at Angaston. About 90 per cent of the grapes they crush are purchased from grape farmers in the valley.

Saltram's have achieved results with the combined talents of Brian Dolan, general manager of the holding company, H. M. Martin and Son, and Peter Lehman. Peter, who is manager and winemaker at Saltram's, has kept abreast of modern winemaking developments and, where finance has permitted, incorporated the latest and most sophisticated equipment for the handling of the whites. This included refrigeration, suitable presses and blanketing of the must and wine with carbon dioxide.

The acquisition by Dalgety's of Martin's and Saltram's has enabled Peter to purchase for the group even more excellent equipment for fermenting whites under controlled pressure conditions.

Peter Lehman spent his early years of winemaking at Yalumba, renowned for their superb Carte d'Or Riesling and nowadays for the famed Pewsey Vale whites. One can follow the improvement of Saltram's wines as, over the

Top: Temperature controlled fermentation vats are a part of contemporary winemaking processes.
Lower: Large oak storage casks at Stanley Wine Co., Clare, S.A.

At vintage time, most small vineyards rely on hand picking. Increasingly, however, the larger vineyards are adapting for machine harvesting which requires a different planting technique.

years, Peter was able to incorporate Yalumba techniques into his winemaking. His own ideas and forceful character impressed themselves on the operation of the winery to such an extent that Saltram's reds and whites, while very much in line with top quality wines elsewhere in Australia, have the distinctive 'Lehman' fingerprints which make them so identifiable.

Probably the most interesting Lehman quirk is his use of the white grape variety, tokay, in the making of the burgundy style of red. This offsets the heavier character of the red shiraz.

Naturally he employs the now well accepted practice of early picking to lessen the 'porty' character of the old Saltram reds. He claims that tokay and also, for that matter, semillon gave a somewhat lighter red with a touch of finesse. Whatever the feelings of more traditional wine-makers in this respect, the practice has been fully vindicated and Saltram burgundies enjoy a good long life and improve tremendously with years of bottle age.

Lehman's white burgundy is distinctive because of his practice of using three varieties, including tokay, crushing and fermenting them together.

Yalumba winery is magnificent. After you have driven into the driveway for the first time you think you have made a mistake and entered the grounds of one of those huge and gracious estates that are scattered here and there in South Australia, and which usually turn out to be the residence of some past governor. A great central clock tower dominates the beautiful old building which is built of local stone.

Yalumba, which is owned by the Hill Smith family, is an example of the enormous growth that has occurred in the Australian wine industry in the last ten years. A thorough look at what is in the company – vineyards, winery and stock – shows an asset position of well over $10 million. Twenty-five years ago, such a figure would have purchased a large slice of the whole Australian wine producing industry.

The Hill Smiths, though a modest and humble family,

are happy with the way things have shaped for them. Every year they invest more and more in their company – new French oak casks bought, more vineyards planted; a cavernous bottling room and completely new bottling line constructed.

Yalumba has a high reputation for its ports – **Galway Pipe** being one of the most sought after and most difficult to obtain in Australia. It is a tawny and therefore aged in casks.

At Yalumba such casks are called puncheons, that is they are about 100 gallons' (455 litres') capacity. They are made either of Nevers or Troncais oak and are used for both red table wines and port.

It is fascinating to observe the process of the ageing of port. From concrete tanks and hardwood casks of 4546 litre capacity, or greater, they are transferred to these puncheons, hundreds of them in one huge cellar. The largest section of the cellar is devoted to **Four Crown Port**. This is only a few years old and there is obviously no shortage of it. Then a smaller section is devoted to **Director's Special Port**; still no shortage by the look of it. Finally, what seems to be a pitifully small section is given up to **Galway Pipe** – specially selected material, very old and the cream of the ports in the cellar.

In recent years Yalumba has been concentrating on high quality table wines. Naturally most of their production results from grapes purchased from local growers, but they do own several hundred acres of vines both in the surrounding hills and at Qualco on the Murray.

In addition, their well publicized partnership with grazier George Angas Parsons at Pewsey Vale is beginning to pay off. Here, 485 metres up in the Barossa Ranges, Parsons owns the land and Yalumba cultivate the grapes. About 80 hectares are devoted to rhine riesling, semillon and cabernet. The climate is greatly different at Pewsey Vale from that down in the Valley. Rainfall is much higher at 812 mm and frosts are more frequent. However, a far more elegant wine has been expected from the grapes and the first vintages have been watched very carefully.

The first, **1964 Yalumba Rhine Riesling**, was a non-eventful white wine, being somewhat uninteresting. **1965**, **1966** and **1967** were a little better. **1968** was comparatively light in flavour and body, but nevertheless showed much of the delicacy and fruit that Yalumba were looking for. **1969** was the white wine we had hoped for. Full flavoured, fruity middle palate, tremendous nose and firm body put it among the great white wines of Australia.

Probably no other wine firm in Australia has had more success in recent years with its white wines than **Leo Buring Pty Ltd**. A curious company is Leo Buring's. Unlike so many of its contemporaries there is no outstanding or flamboyant personality who directs its activities. Instead of the panache and glamour of the old established wine families, there is merely the solid devotion of hard working company executives who command no particular attention. Their company's shareholders should be eternally grateful because they converted a rather difficult financial situation facing the company not so many years ago into one of promise.

The only reason the shareholders do not show their gratitude is that they form a company themselves – Lindeman's in fact; but I suppose Lindeman's shareholders are vicariously and eternally grateful.

At the top of Lindeman's is managing director Ray Kidd, brilliant both as a winemaker and administrator. Stuart Craig heads Leo Buring's and directs operations from Sydney. Reg Shipster is the captain at the winery situated at Tanunda in the Barossa Valley. It is these three solid, hard working and immensely clever men who are mainly responsible for the great whites and reds which emanate from the rather grim, grey winery in the Valley.

Let us look at the Lindeman-Buring system. The grapes are tipped into a fully automated open air pit equipped with fluted crushers, overflow pumps, speed controls, intercom to the inside of the winery and gauges of all kinds. Liquid sulphur dioxide is added to the crushing to inhibit wild yeasts and bacteria and to slow down the effects of oxidation. The must is pumped underground to the winery where it is immediately coated with carbon dioxide, and the arch enemy, fresh air, has no possible chance of getting through.

Buring's use what is called the 'Lindeman' pre-drainer. This is higher than the 'Mac' and in addition gives the must a gas cover. Juice from the white grapes is fed from the pre-drainer into a stainless steel fermenter which is precharged with carbon dioxide pressure, to settling tanks under gas to bottling under gas and ultimately to us the consumers; or to the wine judges for their assessment. These latter gentlemen invariably look at the golden green colour and taste the pure clear liquid and allot it gold medals by the vat-full. Of the remaining skins from the pre-drainer which are still full of precious juice, the top grade material like rhine riesling and Clare riesling go to the Wilmes press. Other material is passed to the continuous, four-stage 'Mac' press which can handle 40·6 tonnes an hour. Thus, there are several qualities of white wine being produced from different grape varieties and by varying processes.

Buring's are also famous today for their red wines. The pre-drainer is by-passed and the crushed red grapes are sent (under gas) immediately to huge stainless steel tanks where they are fermented until sufficient colour is taken from the skins. The skins are pumped away to a Wilmes press where the still fermenting juice is extracted and led into another tank to complete fermentation. The winemaker ultimately decides what shall be blended among the various wines made from myriad sources – free run wine, pressed wine, cabernet grapes, cabernet pressed with shiraz, straight shiraz, and wine from every other type of red grapes that come in.

The Barossa Valley and its surrounding areas is literally crowded with good winemakers these days, each one of them producing excellent products which I have been able to classify as 'great' or 'very great'.

Perhaps the separation of a small district which we call the 'Barossa Valley' from the surrounding districts cannot be entirely justified. In point of fact there is not much

difference in the climate among all the area between St
Vincent's Gulf and the Mt Lofty range with Adelaide on the
south and Kapunda on the north. Certainly there are many
variations of soil but in soils which are suitable for grape
growing there is not likely to be much variation in the
quality of wines in this region. As we have demonstrated
elsewhere, height above sea level affects quality and hence
a difference can be seen between the wines grown in the hills
and those grown on the flats.

The Adelaide environs area which others call Adelaide
Metropolitan, must soon disappear. For obvious reasons,
a vineyard cannot exist in a city where it is surrounded by
homes and shopping areas.

As seen from the lists appearing on pp. 22–48 the
following winemakers of this region, additional to those
mentioned before, have been found worthy of special
recommendation: **Kies**, **Wolf Blass**, **Thomas Hardy & Sons**,
Basedow, **Norman**, **Bernkastel**, **Douglas A. Tolley**, **Stonyfell**
and **Glenview**.

Barossa Ranges

The wineries of the Barossa region can be approached from
several directions. I like best the Main North Eastern road.
As you drive from Adelaide you can inspect, if you wish,
the vineyards of **Wynn's** and **Douglas A. Tolley** at Modbury.
With some surprise you realize that they are not far from the
shopping centre of this little township and that the mammoth
supermarket here, if it were a little larger, might be part of
the vineyards. Further along the road you pass the attractive
little winery of **Angove's** at Tea Tree Gully. You will drive
past the sometimes beautiful Chain of Ponds which in a
wet year is a string of wide beautiful lakes, and in a dry is
simply a few shallow pools. Very quickly you will climb to
the ridge of the Mt Lofty range, and here there are vineyards
all around you if you care to go in search of them. Pewsey
Vale is away to the left and the Steingarten vineyard of
Gramp's can be seen in the distance on a peak overlooking

the Barossa Valley. Still on top of the range, you will find your way through Springton and Eden Valley to Keyneton. All this time you have been travelling through a very beautiful and fertile land. At Keyneton you can take a turn to the east and travel to Nildottie on the Murray River where Hamilton's have an irrigated vineyard.

Cyril Henschke, the winemaker at Keyneton in the hills, has built a name for himself with his highly acid and very dry rieslings. His **White Frontignac**, first of the many, is so well made that it is almost impossible for the average wine drinker to pick the grape variety. An intelligent, alert man, alive to trends in wine drinking, and supremely conscious of the importance of 'good name', Mr Henschke has been able to keep pace with the giants in the State, and in many cases to be one step ahead of them.

Hamilton's with wineries and vineyards at Eden Valley, Springton and Nildottie, seem to have a major interest in this part of Australia. Although not regarded as being in the top size category, Hamilton's have been growing larger over the years, and I greatly suspect that shortly they will emerge with a 'giant' image. Undoubtedly they have made most of their way with the palate-pleasing **Ewell Moselle** which they placed on the market over forty years ago. Hamilton's claim that they were the first to make a wine by the 'closed head' fermentation method. They picked their grapes early in order to retain natural acidity and used closed wooden storage vats as fermenters. The result was a light delicate table wine of a style not previously known in Australia. Ewell Moselle was then and is now made from pedro and verdelho grapes grown at Glenelg. Hamilton's explain that, prior to this, Australian whites were big in style and dark in colour since they were matured in wood in the same way as port and sherry.

It is odd, therefore, that Hamilton's today mature all their white table wines in 160 litre casks of French and American oak. Obviously this gives them more flavour and character than those aged only in stainless steel and glass. Whether the riesling style is thereby improved is perhaps a matter for discussion. Certainly the lovely **Springton White Burgundy** benefits from the wood. It is made from white hermitage grapes, and, in addition to its cask ageing, benefits tremendously from a long period in bottle.

The Hamilton's Springton wines are receiving most favourable recognition by discerning wine drinkers. **The Hermitage**, a dry red made in this area, reaches occasionally for the heights. It is usually highly acid at first, but in a few years it softens and presents itself as a full soft wine with a touch of spice.

Hamilton's **Springton White Frontignac**, which is one of my favourites, is vintaged at the Springton Cellars, from frontignac grapes grown in the adjacent vineyards.

The Barossa Ranges, that section of the Mt Lofty Range which borders the Barossa Valley on the east truly deserves to be classified as a very great area. For as long as I have been drinking wine, the fine crisp white wines made from grapes grown in this area have struck me as the best of the 'riesling' styles made in Australia. The records of the wine shows are an overwhelming indication of the view of our best judges that, in this style, it produces our best rieslings, consistently and in quantity. Our wine writers are lyrical about the beauties of these whites and most of our top ranking amateur wine men agree that they compare with the best whites from other countries.

There are very few wineries actually located in the ranges. Henschke at Keyneton and Hamilton's at Springton and Eden Valley make wine from the local grapes. The bulk of the crop, in fact, goes to the large winemakers in the Valley – Yalumba, Gramp's, Kaiser Stuhl, Buring's and Hardy's. Some undoubtedly is used in blends but the greater percentage of it is sold as straight riesling or semillon as the case may be. Henschke has a small plot of vines at Keyneton, but most of the vines are located in the Springton/Eden Valley region. Yalumba, in conjunction with Mr Geoffrey Angas Parsons, has about 160 hectares of land capable of being planted out to vines at Pewsey Vale and Orlando has a very small plantation of about 1·6 hectares on the highest peak above their winery called 'Steingarten'.

To be strictly correct geographically, we should include the low slopes of the ranges such as those around Angaston and those above Rowland Flat. In these cases temperature is the determining factor. Barossa Ranges grapes are at heights ranging from 365 metres to 487 metres above sea level and the colder climate results in slower ripening of the grapes and a harvesting of the crop some time after grapes in the valley have been picked.

Like anyone else, I have special preferences for certain Barossa Ranges wines. The fruitier rhine rieslings I like best. Yet one can say that there are very few exceptions in the high quality standard of wines marketed as straight whites from this area. **Hamilton's Springton Riesling** and **White Burgundy**, **Hardy's Siegersdorf Rhine Riesling** and **Eden Moselle**, **Kaiser Stuhl Green**, **Gold** or **Purple Ribbon Rieslings**, **Yalumba Special Vintage Riesling** and their **Carte d'Or**, **Henschke Riesling** and **Mosel** are all superb wines. **Pewsey Vale Rhine Riesling** and **Hock** are held by many wine men to be the best whites in Australia. We should include **Orlando Barossa Rhine Riesling**, their special binnings of **Riesling** and **Moselle** and **Blue Ribbon Spaetlese Riesling** since undoubtedly most of the material used in these wines comes from higher up in the ranges. What is so especially blessed about all of these classical wines is that they are so easy to obtain. Perhaps a few of the **Special Bin** numbers of **Burings** and the **Orlando 'Special Label' Riesling** are difficult most of the time but with such a wealth of magnificent wine available from this region under other labels, one does not miss them or even mind.

This area should produce top quality reds and no doubt it will one day. We have yet to see them in consistent and regular production before we can classify them as outstanding.

Southern Vales

REYNELLA
Walter Reynell & Son is (with Hamilton's) the oldest

winemaker in South Australia. From 1838 until 1970 there has been an unbroken line of Reynells in the company, beginning with John Reynell, who established the winery, and finishing when the Reynell shareholders decided to sell the winemaking operation to Hungerford Hill Ltd (now International Cellars Ltd). The Reynell family still have an interest in the land on which the vines are grown.

With the death of the last male member of the family on active service during the war, the company suffered a severe set back and it did not revive until 1952 when the Haselgrove brothers, Colin and Ron, took a financial and active interest in the business. The man at the helm from that time until the takeover by Hungerford Hill was Colin Haselgrove. He will go down in Australian wine history as one of the great men in the industry.

Undoubtedly Haselgrove was one of the greatest wine-makers Australia has had. Until the takeover, Reynella wines had not featured largely on the scene. They were held in high esteem by those who knew their wines well but only the discerning few seemed to purchase them. The cause, no doubt, was that it was only a small winery and could not hope to compete with larger firms which had several times their production on a national scale.

Colin Haselgrove's particular talents were directed to making distinctive dry reds, elegant dry sherries, soft ports and superfine brandy.

In my opinion, all Reynella lines were unappreciated and underpriced for many years. The **Vintage Reserve Claret** is a beautiful rich wine with tremendous flavour and gives enormous satisfaction. It has not changed in all the years I have known it. It follows no particular style, being unlike any French wine I have tasted or most of the Australian reds, even from nearby districts. For about twenty years I enjoyed it every Monday night with the family roast. It is still the same and the price is ridiculously low. Every now and again Reynell market a straight cabernet sauvignon.

International Cellars Ltd which is funded equally by Hungerford Hill Ltd and Rothman's, has elected to make

The House of Reynell label the main feature in their attack on the wine market. Hence even wines from the Hunter Valley district are sold under the Reynell title.

A leaf has been taken from Lindeman's book by combining wines from the Hunter with those from other areas. The best of these is the **Reynella-Pokolbin Shiraz-Cabernet** which is a blend of cabernet and shiraz from Reynella with shiraz from the Reynell vineyard at Pokolbin in the lower Hunter.

The red wines from the Reynella-McLaren Vale district compare well with other wines of Australia. There is no doubt that the blessed plot of land known as Reynella contributes greatly to the success of the above blend. It is good buying at the price.

Reynell also have vineyards at Wylpena, further south in the McLaren Vale area. Some of this wine goes into the **Bin 2 Claret** blend. Bin 2 has always been, in my opinion, the most underpriced red on the market. It is excellent, a typical product of Colin Haselgrove's genius, and at today's price a bottle should be purchased, laid down and kept for ten years. I am astonished how much this standard wine improves.

Over the years, very old Reynella reds have been produced at the tables of connoisseur groups and invariably they are recognised as being examples of quality Australian reds.

HAPPY AND COROMANDEL VALLEYS

If you travel from the city of Adelaide along the top of the Mt Lofty range to McLaren Vale you can see (just out of the city) the vineyards on the hillsides between the road and the sea. They decorate the slopes as an artist might make up his canvas when he first begins a design, geometrical patterns of straight lines and squares cut into blurs of foliage and bluffs. Colour is splashed on haphazardly – greens and browns, yellows, purples, reds. The many slopes facing east make for quality wines. The soils are rich loams with mixtures of limestone and clays. The vines are healthy and easy to maintain.

The area is cultivated by very many small vignerons who do not wish to make wine themselves and so sell their grapes to wineries nearby. The quality is invariably high and some wines will no doubt be able to be classified as 'outstanding'.

Some of the grape growers have wineries and specialise in making top quality table wines. They are **Pridham** (Marienberg), **Paul** (Trennert), **Light** (Light Wines), **Torresan** (Happy Valley) and **Glenloth**. Reynella I have dealt with separately.

McLaren Vale

McLaren Vale can be approached from several directions. The Onkaparinga River forms the boundary to the north, the Willunga Escarpment to the south; the sea is at the west and the Mt Lofty Ranges at the east.

The approach over the high ridge from Strathalbyn is the most scenic. The vineyards can be seen almost immediately. Some of them are high on the hills; others are tucked away behind the stands of timber. The McLaren Valley is very fertile. On the range, native trees, especially the great gums, decorate the scene with their complicated patterns and eccentric but beautiful branches. Further down the valley, the area presents a different picture every season. In the spring the blossoming apple and peach, the crab-apple and the cherry splash their milky white, their pinks and their cyclamens across the countryside, and the budding vines fold their graceful arms over their austere trellises.

No part of South Australia looks more prosperous. The local stone has been used for building houses and barns and it is still used most effectively. The old houses with their early Victorian architecture, square doorways and windows, and doily-like cast iron trimmed verandahs are as well maintained, painted and restored as any of the ancient palaces of Italy. Their yellows and creams, dark maroons and browns blend well with the deep red clay and green foliage. These rocks and stones are used effectively in the modern houses and imaginative wineries designed both for efficiency and aesthetic appeal.

It is astonishing that until recently, the wine trade has not given McLaren Vale the prominence given to the Barossa Valley. It is a comparatively large agricultural and viticultural area producing well over 4,500 kl of table wines a year. The terrain is beautiful and pleasing to tourists, and the vignerons are as warmhearted and gregarious as those from any other part of South Australia. Above all, the red wines are big, soft and pleasing.

Ben Chaffey's **Seaview Vineyard** is the highest in the valley. It is now owned by Toohey's of Sydney.

The **Ryecroft** vineyard and winery has been sold to Reed Paper Products. Ryecroft had been owned by the Ingoldby family since 1919. A little while ago it amalgamated with McLaren Vale Wine Pty Ltd of which Jim Ingoldby and Ege Dennis were shareholders. The assets of both companies, therefore, were sold to the Reed Group.

The soils of McLaren Vale are extremely varied. One would naturally expect this because some of them are on the hills and some are on the flats.

At Seaview with its 80 odd hectares of vines, ironstone impregnated gravel predominates in the top soil which is shallow. The subsoil is a chalk impregnated soft marl. Next door to Seaview is **Kay's Amery** vineyard where the soil is mostly sandy loam with some ironstone boulders and the subsoil is clay. **Coriole** on the opposite side of the road is similar.

Down the hills towards McLaren Flat lies **Osborn's D'Arenberg** vineyard, again with soil similar to that of Kay's.

Ryecroft vineyard down on the flats is on red clay and sandy loam. At **Johnston's Pirramimma** vineyard across the railway line the soil varies from sand on the high rises to Biscay loam in the hollows.

Yet with all this variety of soil there is an overall sameness of flavour in the reds of the area.

The appearance in recent years of **Hardy's McLaren Vale Hermitage** and more recently of their **Nottage Hill Claret** is an indication of the Hardy family's acknowledgement of the growing awareness of the public of the name McLaren Vale. Burgoyne's of London have been associated with Hardy's from the early days of winemaking in South Australia. Millions of gallons of Hardy's wines have been sold in England through Burgoyne's.

The Emu Wine Company, Stephen Smith and Gilbey's have been big buyers for the English market of the heavy McLaren Vale reds. The export trade has decreased but perhaps the English companies buying wineries in the area are more calculating than we thought at first.

The older one becomes the more clearly it appears that we must always keep our options open. In the world of wine it is, as some philosophers say, a world of becoming, of constant change. One learns never to be too definite, too sure, too dogmatic. Contrariwise, we shrewdly adopt the attitude that we are learning something new about wine every day. Even preconceived notions held for many years eventually crumble and give way to new ideas. That is a general statement and should not be taken as a direct reference to the following comments.

The McLaren Vale area of South Australia is of late gaining some reputation as a producer of high class table wines. There is no viticultural or oenological reason of which I am aware that should prevent first class table wine being made in this area. The fact that it has not been given due acknowledgement as a classic area is a fault that lies, no doubt, in the grape varieties grown and the methods of the winemakers in former years.

The few awards that have been granted to this region at recent wine shows do not necessarily indicate that it is already a famed table wine area. Reputations are gained, not from the inconsistent and sometimes random assessment of varied and varying wine judges at our multiplicity of wine fairs, but from the constant approval over many years of experienced amateurs of wine. In this sense, an amateur, is intended to mean a person who has a taste for a particular art. The slow, thoughtful appreciation of a different wine every day builds up a mental picture of what wines are great, what are good and those not worth the time. I consider the skilled wine amateur's assessment far more valuable as a guide to the quality of a wine than any hasty judgements by show judges under various pressures.

In recent years one cannot but be aware of some of the magnificent bottlings of **Hardy's** made from straight Southern Vales material. Their **McLaren Vale Cabernet Sauvignon** is undoubtedly a classic.

Some of Seaview straight cabernet reds, especially those made in the early sixties, are outstanding and an indication that quality wines can be made consistently in McLaren Vale.

D'Arry Osborn seems to have replaced some of his older vines with more suitable table wine varieties and one or two of his reds and whites, in their own distinctive and highly individual style qualify for the title of 'great'.

The Ingoldby vineyard, **Ryecroft**, tradition maker of heavy fully flavoured reds has, in recent years, come up with a lighter, more refined claret style red which has reached the heights.

Influences such as this must surely bring this district into line with other classic areas of Australia.

In the middle of 1972 a bottle of dry red arrived mysteriously on my table apparently sent from some small, unknown winemaker in South Australia. I placed it in the bin of wines which I keep to be tasted 'blind'. Eventually it came up among a batch of wines which included a Redman Coonawarra. On reading my notes after the tasting, I found that I had commented: 'The colour is violet; the nose is perfumed and lovely; the palate has a most attractive approach, the middle showing a nice spicy flavour. There is a presence of beautiful French oak, good acid and good tannin . . . a well above average wine of great appeal with good ageing potential'. On reflection when the wine was unwrapped, I thought how similar in style it was to the Redman. I noted that it was a sample bottle of 1970 shiraz made by Dr Hugh Lloyd. The wine had not yet been bottled and the sample had been drawn from the cask.

A few weeks later I was in Adelaide and I visited Dr Lloyd, a busy general medical practitioner. Together we set off for McLaren Vale to his vineyard which he had named **Coriole**, and we looked at the wines he had made, all of which were still in cask.

The 1970 shiraz tasted very much as had the sample which Dr Lloyd had sent me. Here are my comments on the 1971 wines: '**Shiraz 1971 No. 1.** The colour is a very deep purple. The bouquet is pleasingly perfumed. On the palate the oak is very pronounced but the flavour matches it well; a really lovely wine which at this stage is showing too much Nevers oak character.' **Shiraz 1971 No. 2.** 'The nose has more fruit but less oak. On the palate the oak is less but still obvious. The tannin and fruit balance is excellent.' (I recommended to Dr Lloyd that he put both wines together to reduce the excessive French oak flavour in No. 1.) **Shiraz-cabernet 1971 No. 3.** 'Magnificent purple colour. The nose has a combination of wonderful aromas, fruit and oak. On the palate the oak is very strong. The middle palate is magnificent and the finish good. There is not as much fruit showing as in the straight shiraz but this should be corrected with age.' Only 12 per cent of this wine is cabernet but it is enough to impart a Bordeaux style of early-life hardness and a deeper character.

Evidently Dr Lloyd followed my suggestion with the 1971 shiraz. The oak flavour is not nearly as obtrusive as it was in the No. 1 cask. The wine has many flavour characteristics not present in the 1970. I hope to see it in ten years' time. It should be superb.

'Coriole' consists only of a few hectares of vineyards situated on the sloping hillside 6·5 km north of the town of McLaren Vale. Nearby, Seaview and Kay's have planted some hundreds of hectares. The reputation of these two latter wineries undoubtedly derives from the microclimate of this higher part of the valley, which seems to assist in the birth of outstanding dry reds and whites.

Hugh and Molly Lloyd with two partners acquired both the vines and the new winery in 1969. The old ironstone cottage built in 1860 has been converted into an attractive 'cellar-door' sales area. Hugh Lloyd is highly scientific in his approach and takes no steps without first consulting experts like Bryce Rankine and Owen Redman. I am quite certain that, soon, Coriole reds will take their place among the outstanding wines of Australia.

Those of us who can go back only ten years in the history of Australian wine drinking will not be able to recall any national wine firm marketing a wine simply as 'McLaren Vale'. I am fairly certain that the first Hardy 'McLaren Vale Hermitage' was not marketed until 1966.

Why the shyness of a large company like Thomas Hardy and Sons in making a feature of the area where they loomed largest on the scene? The answer might lie in the fact that for a period of time the great Hardy concern was dedicated to a theory known as 'blending to a standard'. This hypothesis called for the blending of various wines from all over Australia in order that every year a similarity of style, flavour, weight and colour could be achieved. The wonderful Old Castle Rieslings, Cabinet Clarets and St Thomas Burgundies of an earlier era were a tribute to the blending skill of Hardy's who used Hunter Valley, Barossa Valley, Victoria and their own McLaren Vale vineyards to synthesize consistent and high quality wines every year.

Yet all this tended to lower the prestige of this southern area. If the great Hardy family was not featuring McLaren Vale in its advertising and on its labels, then who amongst the smaller makers would dare to do so?

There must have been some murmurings of discontent among the southern firms in the early sixties when wine really began to become big business. Now the Hunter and the Barossa became household words. Even Tahbilk, Rutherglen and Great Western were firmly established names among Australia's wine drinkers; but McLaren Vale? Where was that?

Strangely, the wines made in the valleys south of Adelaide had always been sought after by the large companies operating in the more famous regions. Their great bodied reds with their deep intense colour and huge flavour contributed greatly to blends made up basically with wines from areas not so well blessed with these characteristics.

Modern wine technology showed the McLaren Vale winemakers that they need not always produce great heavy, astringent wines. The area could bring forth lighter, more balanced and easier to drink wines while still possessing the full flavour of the south.

Hardy's McLaren Vale Hermitage was a success. Then Ege Dennis and Jim Ingoldby stirred the smaller growers into making a bid for identity. McLaren Vale has now arrived as one of the glamour areas of wine growing in Australia with highly distinctive dry reds as its mainstay.

The Hardy family followed up McLaren Vale Hermitage with straight **McLaren Vale Cabernet** which proved outstandingly successful. Then came, in the late sixties, **'Nottage Hill'**, a dry red made from grapes grown on a Hardy property right near the township after which the district is named. This was the peak of Hardy technique in handling the shiraz grape.

Even in the past few years winemaking techniques have improved in an extraordinary way. The mastering of the method of ageing dry reds in new French or American oak has been the most remarkable development.

Recently, as my colleagues and I were having our usual weekly tasting of wines, someone remarked how frequently a top quality red among those we tasted turned out to be from McLaren Vale. It seems to us that a greater quantity of consistently high class reds comes from McLaren Vale every year. For some unknown reason, of late the weekly tastings have included different wines from a winery almost unknown outside South Australia. It is called **Valle D'Oro**, or used to be. Today it is known as **Golden Valley Winery**.

One begins to understand why we see so many wines from McLaren Vale when it is discovered that the total storage at Golden Valley is 1545·6 kl, of which 454·6 kl is underground. The winery was first built in 1929 and, not surprisingly, was used until about 1946 for the storage of port. The vats are still used but now only dry red is stored in them. Perhaps that is the reason that the reds of Valle D'Oro have such a rich character.

In 1964 two young men, Giordanno Rossetto and Lorenzo Commazzetto, purchased the then largely disused cellars. In a remarkably short time they developed it into one of the largest winemaking units in the McLaren Vale area. These two men learned how to make wine and in the beginning were the only winemakers. Soon they realized the importance of having a professional in charge of this operation and appointed Anthony Vucasovich, who was trained in Europe, to the position in 1968.

Very quickly, stainless steel storage casks, a 2000 gallon (9·09 kl) pressure fermenter, refrigeration equipment and modern bottling, corking and labelling machinery were introduced. Thus, in a few years the partnership developed a run down concern into one of the most sophisticated and efficient wineries in South Australia. In June 1970 a further 32·37 hectares of land adjacent to the winery were purchased and planted with cabernet sauvignon and shiraz, although, naturally, for such large production most grapes are purchased from local growers.

One can understand why large public companies are entering the wine field. Wine consumption the whole world over has increased at such an enormous rate that, from a capital appreciation point of view, there can be very few industries to equal it. In addition it does not seem to suffer the same vicissitudes in short periods as other primary industries.

No wonder then that Dalgety's snapped up the opportunity of taking over Valle D'Oro Winery in June 1971. This company later purchased H. M. Martin and Son (including both the Stonyfell and Saltram operations) and the old Falkenberg Winery (now called Glenview).

Prosperity in the wine trade increases and wanes in large cycles and no doubt at one time or other in the future we shall see financial difficulties for the industry as a whole. To take a long term view, however, any investment in wine can only be wise. Dalgety's have purchased three excellent and prestigious operations. Their shareholders will benefit in the future.

Until recently much of the wine sold by Valle D'Oro was sold to larger companies for marketing under their labels. Some of it went to large scale operations like Agostino and the Vintage Club in Melbourne where acknowledgement on the label would be given to the makers. No doubt these outlets will be used for many years until Valle D'Oro's own label is established. It seems that this will be under the title of **'Roxton Estate'** in commemoration of the original label used by the first builders of the winery.

Whatever the case, I am impressed by their wines. No doubt there will be the usual troubles associated with rapid acceleration of production but, basically, the area is good and the wines are well made.

LANGHORNE CREEK

Langhorne Creek has always seemed to me to be an unlikely place for the growing of vines. Yet it is obviously a small area that plays an important part in the total enactment of the Australian wine game. 'Game' is almost an exact word to describe the activities of winemakers and grapegrowers because they can never be sure what the outcome of their efforts will be; nor can they ever comprehend the outside influences that decide whether they win or not – weather, the support of their followers, the rules of officials, luck.

At all events, Langhorne Creek red wine is considered by at least one company to be the best it markets, and the vats of Langhorne Creek winemakers are constantly raided by the largest companies for wines which are used in blends. Their full flavour and usually good colour fill out and give more density to vintages from other areas lacking in these qualities.

Lindeman's and Penfold's are good customers and have marketed outstanding wines either as blends or as straight reds from Langhorne Creek.

The Potts family owns the only winery in the area. They
call it **Bleasdale** after the reverend gentleman of that name
who earned a reputation for himself last century in Australia
by preaching the daily consumption of wine as an answer to
the problem of alcoholism. John Potts and his four sisters,
great-grandchildren of the founder, Frank, still run the
winery. When the Bremer flows they lower a homemade
weir constructed of a sheet of iron across the stream. This
causes the Bremer to overflow its banks and to flood the
240 hectares or so of vineyards at Langhorne Creek. Usually
this provides enough moisture to sustain the vines throughout the summer and vintage; but it is odd to see only the
tops of the vines peeping out of the water. It is another
example of the Australian ability to improvise.

The soil near the creek is a heavy black alluvial loam.
Some of the vineyards are on the red sand further away.

The Potts own about 40 hectares of the vineyards but
most of them are the property of independent growers who
farm the land in several ways. H. M. Martin and Sons
have about another 40 hectares and from the vineyards
of Denys Butler, known as **Metala**, come the cabernet
grapes which make the famous wine of the same name.

Until recently the Potts' winery produced a prepon-
derance of sweet fortified wines which they made from the
shiraz, malbec, palomino, pedro and frontignan grapes
that grow in the area. More recently they have used these
grapes to make dry wines such as **Frontignac Dry White**
and **Malbec Dry Red**.

The sweet fortified wines enjoy lovely old titles like
Constantia and **Verdielho**. In the early days of our history
sailing ships would call in at Cape Colony in South Africa
and sometimes pick up a few vines for the South Australian
winemakers like Frank Potts. Constantia is a type of
muscat grape and produces a luscious, extremely fruity and
rich dessert wine. The Verdielho was transplanted in South
Africa from the island of Madeira, and Potts' make it into
a syrupy full wine without the strong flavour of the original
Portuguese wine.

South-east South Australia

COONAWARRA

Although Coonawarra is a comparatively small area, there are many winemakers who either make wine there or who use the grapes to make wine in their wineries many miles away. Wynn's, Redman's, Rouge Homme (Lindeman's), Mildara, Penfold's and Brand make Coonawarra reds while Hardy's and Woodley's buy it, give it their own cellar treatment and bottle it. Because of a difference of opinion regarding vintaging among these makers, we cannot accurately describe the wine of any of them as a 'typical' Coonawarra. In fact there are *two* Coonawarras, because there are two basic styles.

I often attend wine dinners where I hear our top wine men confusing Wynn's Coonawarras with top class Bordeaux reds when the wines are served masked. Coonawarra reds are our best red wines with only our top Hunters as possible rivals.

Coonawarras may give occasional let-downs . . . the occasional bad bottling, the over high acidity in youth of some years, the extraordinary volatility almost always present in every bottling of Wynn's from 1950 to 1964, the dead pan flatness of the wine the day after the bottle has been opened, its nondescript character at odd periods of its life, its dumbness in early years of odd vintages. Irrespective of all this I know now that Coonawarra reds of any year will eventually give me more satisfaction than any other Australian red. The faults are temporary or of little significance compared with the magnificence of the wine. In any case they can all be explained away as due to human error. The wine is so good that its excellence will force its way through in spite of them.

Wynn's Coonawarra is representative of the wines of the area because Wynn's has adopted a philosophy of vintaging which they inherited from old John Redman and which is also followed by all other growers in the area except Mildara. There is, therefore, a 'Redman' style and a

'Mildara' style of Coonawarra red.

Without doubt both Coonawarra and Hunter reds can claim equality, under certain conditions, with all but the great wines of the world. These conditions are correct vintaging, great care during fermentation and perfect cellaring. Until recent years these conditions occurred only occasionally and then by accident rather than by design.

A combination of scientific knowledge, supplied by the Australian Wine Research Institute, and correct thinking, supplied by David Wynn and Ronald Haselgrove, is ensuring that future Coonawarra reds will be perfect. There are two soil varieties at Coonawarra, but this is not the reason for the two different styles of Coonawarra red. Both of these soils are derived from parent limestone and the weathering, leaching and chemical changes have been much the same. Apparently one layer of limestone was harder than another and the resultant top soil developed differently to that derived from the softer limestone.

This latter is a black soil called 'rendzina' and is much more difficult to work than the red. It is almost clay-like in its texture and when wet has a great similarity to putty. Those who are directly concerned therefore with planting vines and fruit trees and working the soil in the rendzina belt are continually frustrated with it and are inclined to be harsh in their judgement of it as compared with the red belt which is known as 'terra rossa'. Terra rossa is friable and more porous.

In the first couple of years vine plants take more easily in the red soil than in the black. Watering is simpler and in every way vine care involves less trouble on the red than it does on the black soil. As one would expect, therefore, vines thrive better on the terra rossa. Bill Redman says that the grapes tend to ripen more slowly on the vines on the black soil than they do on the red.

The lateness of vintaging time due to slower ripening of grapes will necessarily produce a slightly different wine in taste, but I cannot see any difference in quality between wines grown on the red and the black soils. In any case, since winemakers in the area buy their grapes from both sections and crush them together there does not seem to be much point in making the distinction.

Suitable soils make for healthy vines; healthy vines produce good grapes, but the distinctive flavour and quality of wine is due more to climate than to soil. I have no doubt that vines grown in a water solution fed with sufficient nutrient material and situated in the Coonawarra environment would produce exactly the same type of wine as would grapes grown on the limestone soil in the area.

The other predominant factor in the quality of the wine is in the way it is handled, and winemaking is similar to the wooing of a woman – every one is to be treated differently.

I have already intimated that, in my opinion, there are two styles of Coonawarra reds; the Redman style and the Mildara style. This statement, I feel, is true for all vintages at least as far as the 1969 vintage. My preference is for the Redman style, but I am open to conviction and perhaps in the seventies we shall see a merging of the two different types. If this happens it will mean that we shall see a better wine all round; because, despite my great love for the Redman style of Coonawarra, there are deficiencies in both styles. These should be quickly removed so that we can have a top quality red equivalent to the best reds of France.

The beauty of the old-style Redman type red is its similarity to the Bordeaux wines of France. To depart from this style and similarity would, in my opinion, be a mistake. The earlier Mildara reds, in spite of their undoubted excellence, did in fact depart from the style of Bordeaux. The drawback of the Redman style, however, is its high acidity in youth, the time it takes to age, and a lacking of full Bordeaux flavour in the middle palate while it is young. The drawback of the earlier Mildara style according to my palate is its over-fullness of flavour and body at an early age and a too great and aggressive oak tannin.

The **1963 Mildara Straight Cabernet Sauvignon** won almost as many gold medals as the 1962 Grange Hermitage.

This may have convinced the makers that they were on the right track. There is no denying that the wine was first class but, in my book, it fell down as a first class Coonawarra. Its fault was that it lacked a Bordeaux character. It was too rich and the sharp Medoc sting on the lips and first palate was missing. Mildara Coonawarra reds have more or less been like that ever since: rich, fruity, flavorous wines with plenty of oak character, but lacking the refinement of a top Bordeaux.

If the object of the winemaker is to produce a typical first rate Australian style red, then undoubtedly he has succeeded and such a wine should sell well to a market already conditioned to this style of wine. Hunter Valley makers will be the only competitor for they, at this point of time, are also producing top quality Australian reds, full of flavour, rich and soft.

This is, perhaps, where traditional Redman style Coonawarra makers are missing out. The Australian public does not very much like a highly acid red. It is slow to acquire a liking for French-type wines which are different from our own.

But in addition to this, the Redman makers are as yet missing the point. Their wines are ready for drinking only after five years at least. They must, like the makers of Bordeaux, learn to combine the qualities of highly refined acid with fullness of flavour in youth. Thus the wines will be ready for drinking two or three years after making, even though they possess the quality to enable them to age for many years.

A compromise or a rapprochement between the two styles is necessary.

Vignerons and winemakers in this area will no doubt have their arguments against my thesis and perhaps be able to throw out minor points of my reasoning. Yet I believe that at least one firm is taking steps to achieve a closer line-up between its Coonawarra wines and top French Bordeaux, and that is Wynn's (the Coonawarra Estate Company). In the long run, I suppose, it is a matter of company policy. Does the company want to produce wines that are similar to top chateau-bottled wines of France, or does it want to make wines which are distinctively Australian and, even so, top quality in their own way.

If it can, I believe Coonawarra should almost slavishly follow the Bordeaux-Medoc makers. There are other places such as Hunter Valley and McLaren Vale where we can develop typical Australian styles, but at Coonawarra we have the opportunity of making a red which will compare equally with the already accepted best wines in the world and ease the export position of our quality reds. Wynns Winemakers Limited in 1970 used pressings in their wines for the first time. Until then they had used no new oak wood in their wines except for a little in their Cabernet Sauvignon.

The Redman-style winemakers are **Wynn's**, **Rouge Homme**, **Owen Redman**, **Penfold's** and **Brand**. They follow the traditional methods laid down by Bill Redman who, with over fifty years of winemaking, ought to know the rules of good wine making. The Mildara style of Coonawarra was dictated by Mr Ronald Haselgrove, managing director of that company, and his chief winemaker, Syd Wells. They adhere strictly to viticultural methods as set out by the latest exponents of scientific theory on grape growing. One would imagine, therefore, that their example would be more readily followed by the others. The fact that it is not is due to the climate of Coonawarra.

The difference between the two theories is viticultural. Actual winemaking methods are much the same except for a variation in the use of oak. Wine science has evened all other differences.

The grape grower at Coonawarra is faced with many problems. His first real difficulty is to have his grapes sufficiently ripened before the autumn rains set in. Admittedly, he does not have this difficulty on his own. Many a crop has been ruined in other districts because of rain. However, the Coonawarra grape grower has to wait longer

Coonawarra is always in dread of rain. Yet so many other climatic factors are closely aligned – the pattern of average summer temperature; heat summation; total sun hours. Bordeaux begins to pick during the latter half of the second month of autumn. If Coonawarra growers waited for the same Baume degree of sugar, they would also begin to pick towards the end of the second month of autumn. We could then, at Coonawarra, well follow the example of the Bordelaise. 'Thanks to the introduction of the Control of Grape Maturation, the vigneron is from now on freed from the care of deciding himself the exact moment of the vintage. The Control of Grape Maturation permits also the determination of the best compromise between the dates of maturity of the different grape varieties. The date of the vintage depends on the type of wine desired. If it is a question of dry wine, the grape will be vintaged before full maturation in order to preserve an agreeable acidity'. (*Dictionnaire des Vins*, Larousse.)

The date of vintage is no longer set by a committee of wine makers in Bordeaux but the principle mentioned in the above paragraph is still followed by individual chateaux. The Medoc grower has the advantage of being able to call on a great number of grape pickers who can harvest his crop within a few days of the selected date. Perhaps the Coonawarra companies are too ambitious. Their vineyards are too large to enable them to gather in their crops quickly once the day of vintage has been decided. It should not be too difficult to solve a problem of that nature. If pickers are scarce, mechanical harvesting might be considered.

Whatever the errors that are being committed, it is only a matter of time before the problems are solved. These problems belong to the winegrowing and winemaking companies. It is up to them to find the solutions.

I love the Wynn-Redman Coonawarra wines now. The older they become, the more I like them, but they are not yet perfect. With a little change in operations, I am sure they could become almost identical with top Medoc wines, provided they are not given too much oak and the flavour is allowed to come from the grape. If there are one or two bad seasons where the vigneron loses his crop because of weather conditions, let him charge more, as the French do, for the great wines he will be presenting in the good years. I, for one will be prepared to pay for them.

KEPPOCH

Without doubt, the most enterprising of all new vineyard projects in recent years has been that of the Keppoch Valley. I feel sure the name has been coined by Seppelt's. There are no surface streams in the area and, although there is a low range of hills to the north, it enjoys the name of *Valley* only by courtesy.

The town of Naracoorte lies close to the Victorian – South Australian border; a road leads from Naracoorte to Keith and on this road there is a mythical place which appears on the map as Keppoch. 14·5 kilometres further is the tiny township of Padthaway. Between these two spots is a stretch of land 1·6 kilometres wide which is singularly blessed by a combination of factors that are entirely lacking in the entire surrounding area.

First there is a layer of friable loam, red brown earth in soil type. Below this there is a band of good red clay and beneath this again there is limestone. The annual rainfall is about 585 mm but, as though this were not enough, there is an underground water supply which seems limitless. It appears that this is being constantly renewed by underground streams. The build up of solids is minimal, being only fifty-eight parts per million. Around Padthaway the grass is high, sheep and cattle look well fed and contented and the great red gums give an indication as to the fertility of the soil.

Seppelt's began planting vines here about 1964. Several vintages have been experienced and Seppelt's winery men report that the cabernets are of high quality. They have won a medal every year so far. The Hermitage, too, is of a high standard and the Rhine Riesling has been winning medals.

As the water table at present is only 3·7 metres below the surface, most varieties of grapes will get their roots to it. Seppelt's engage in irrigation only to enhance vine flowering and to fill out the berries after Christmas. The area cannot therefore be regarded as irrigated. It would be more correct to describe the procedure as supplementary watering. In very dry years the underground supply will be a real boon. A pull of a switch and thousands of litres an hour come bursting up, sufficient to flood irrigate a vineyard in a very short time.

Thomas Hardy and Sons have their project well under way. The company has 120 hectares in the area, most of them producing. Several of the cabernets and cabernet shiraz blends have won gold medals.

Glenloth, which is a Tooheys Ltd subsidiary, is developing many hundreds of hectares at Keppoch. This is a new turn for Glenloth since, up to this time, they have had no vineyards of their own. For many years they have purchased grapes for their winery situated at Reynella and this new project will probably upgrade their name to one of some prominence.

Finally, **Lindeman's** have purchased 809 hectares.

Prior to the Second World War the whole district was bare, uninhabited and almost desert like. Scientists decided that the addition of so-called trace elements would improve the soil. In those days a shilling for half a hectare was considered a fair price for the land. The traces were added but trefoil such as lucerne had to be planted to produce the nitrogen so necessary for the cultivation of crops and grasses. Now the lucerne at Keppoch Valley is being pulled out and replaced by vines. The price of land there has rocketed.

The Murray Valley
Whether irrigation affects the quality of a wine has not been established. Briefly it does indeed appear that quality suffers when vineyards are occasionally heavily flooded because of water rights rather than in response to the

demands of good viticulture. If a vigneron were able to water his vines when they needed water, give them just the right amount of moisture, and to stop the supply just before harvest so that the grapes were not too well plumped, then an irrigated vineyard would be in a better position than one that relied on natural rainfall.

The Murray and Murrumbidgee Irrigation systems do not operate that way. Under their system the water allowance must be used when it is made available otherwise the subscriber loses claim to the allowance. This gives rise to the temptation to take as much water as possible when it is available to be drawn.

Nonetheless, from time to time first quality red wines keep on appearing from these areas.

It seems to me that irrigation of itself is a comparatively small factor affecting the quality of the grapes in the Murray and Murrumbidgee Valleys. The flat terrain and the summer light and heat are the major reasons why these areas do not produced top quality wine.

In the listing of The Wine Areas (p. 1) I have separated the area embracing the towns of Renmark, Loxton, Berri, Barmera and Waikerie (which I have called Northern Murray) from the area around Nildottie (Southern Murray). To my palate there is a difference in the wines from Nildottie.

As this book deals only with the classification of Australian vineyards of a quality of and above 'great' and Murray Valley vineyards are rated only as 'very good,' I do not intend to discuss the various vineyards of this area.

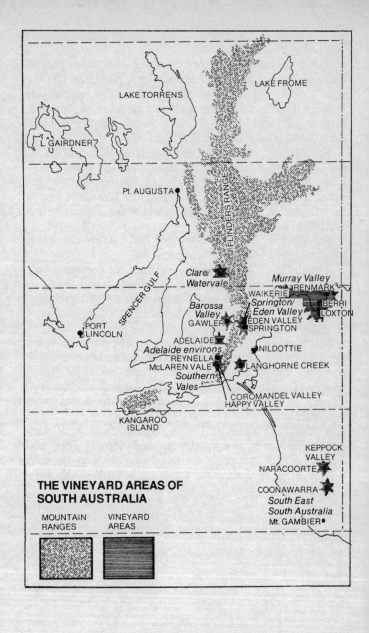

THE VINEYARD AREAS OF
SOUTH AUSTRALIA

MOUNTAIN
RANGES

VINEYARD
AREAS

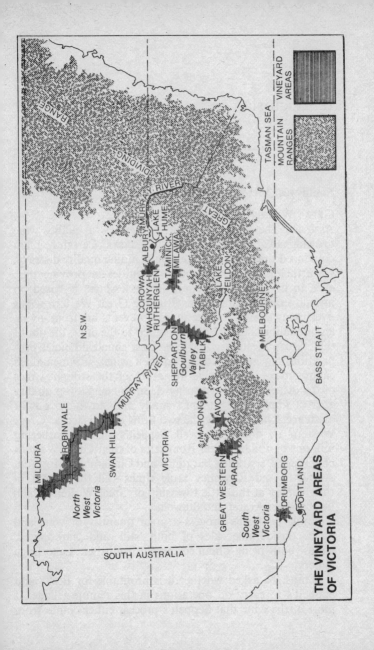

THE VINEYARD AREAS
OF VICTORIA

VINEYARD
AREAS

MOUNTAIN
RANGES

TASMAN SEA

BASS STRAIT

MELBOURNE

N.S.W.

VICTORIA

SOUTH AUSTRALIA

GREAT DIVIDING RANGE

MURRAY RIVER

RIVER

Lake
Hume

ALBURY
COROWA
WAHGUNYAH
RUTHERGLEN

TAMINICK
MILAWA

Lake
Eildon

SHEPPARTON
Goulburn
Valley
TABILK

MARONG
AVOCA

MILDURA
ROBINVALE
SWAN HILL

North
West
Victoria

GREAT WESTERN
ARARAT

DRUMBORG
PORTLAND

South
West
Victoria

6 Victoria

South-west Victoria

GREAT WESTERN – AVOCA – DRUMBORG

Assessing the value of Great Western as a quality wine growing area is not the easiest of tasks. Certainly I am convinced that it is one of our outstanding quality districts. Nevertheless, there are many difficulties in proving this, even to my own satisfaction. My assessment is based on my judgement formed after drinking Great Western wines over many years. Yet one reason prevents me from giving an unqualified stamp of 'top quality' to the area: the doubt that Great Western could ever be a sound financial proposition. No matter how good their wines, if winemakers cannot make a profitable living out of the straight wines of the district, it can never lay claim to being a top quality area of importance. It must surely and slowly go out of existence. Undoubtedly the two firms established at Great Western are doing very well. **Seppelt's** must be gathering millions of dollars a year from sales of their Great Western champagne, sparkling burgundy and Chalambar, Moyston, Arawatta and Rhymney table wines – all the output of their winery at this little township of Great Western which lies between Ararat and Stawell.

Similarly, **Best's** process a great quantity of wine and have considerable sales of both 'still' and 'carbonated' wines, both being obtained largely from their Lake Boga winery.

It must be asked whether it is profitable for Best's and Seppelt's to carry on operations in this remote village. If most of the wine that Seppelt's process either comes from other States or other areas in Victoria, or alternatively is made from grapes grown in these other districts, would it not be more economical for them to establish their winery close to one of their greatest markets, e.g. Melbourne? Would it not be wiser for Best's to close their Great Western winery and to rationalize their production by concentrating their operation at Lake Boga whence comes by far the greatest proportion of their wine?

Thank heavens these are questions I do not have to answer; but the reason that causes me to raise them is sufficient to deter any other potential ventures in that district. However, there may be other places in the same region which will produce just as good quality wines and prove more economical.

I believe that Avoca is one such area. It may be said that in the last few years of boom conditions Great Western has proved extremely profitable to both the large and the small concern. I feel sure that when good wine becomes plentiful all over Australia, as it will very soon, the economic disadvantages of Great Western will reappear.

What are these economic disadvantages? They may be summed up as 'low yield' and 'frost'. Low yield may eventually be overcome. Clone selection of vines, the planting of more suitable varieties, the utilization of improved scientific knowledge in the cultivation of the vine will probably increase yields to a satisfactory level, but how do you overcome a persistent and continuing condition of annual pernicious frosts? Every third or fourth year sees the complete destruction of shoots in the spring frosts which attack all the vineyards on the flats.

Sometimes a second budding saves the situation, but inevitably the result is lower yields and later ripening with attendant difficulties. On the all-too-common occasions when a whole vineyard is unproductive for the year, the crops of the following years would have to be sold at a price two and a half times as great in order to break even. Obviously this is just not possible under normal conditions of demand.

A straight Great Western wine should, consequently, be one of the most expensive wines in Australia. If it were possible to convince consumers that the wines were worth the extra price, possibly Great Western would be economically self sufficient. I doubt, however, that a wine lover would pay twice as much for a Great Western as he would for a Coonawarra.

Seppelt's use their Great Western winery as a centre for their 'prestige' table wines and for the manufacture of their sparkling wines. Wines receiving cellar treatment and bottled here are: **Chalambar Burgundy**, **Moyston Claret**, **Arawatta Riesling**, **Rhymney Chablis**, **Chardonnay Sauternes** and **Melita Moselle**.

Seppelt's make no claim on the labels as to where the wines come from. As there is a general consistency in their character and their overall excellence does not vary from year to year, it is more than probable that the wines of the district are blended with wines of other districts to balance the lack of body and excessive acid which characterizes Great Western wines of a poor year.

In addition, Seppelt's market what are purported to be 'straight' Great Western wines. In most cases the 'straight' reds are lighter in colour than the reds of other great areas. They show a great similarity to the wines of Best's across the road – as indeed they should, since the area is confined to a small circumference. In odd years the red wines of the area are full and fruity and remind me of the wines made by Colin Preece in the forties and fifties. Such full, rich red wines can be made only from fully ripened grapes with a high sugar content and a lessened acidity.

The conditions which permit the grapes to reach this state are very rare in Great Western. Picking of grapes begins sometimes in March if the year is hot, but a fully ripened shiraz grape of a sugar baume of say 13, would have to remain on the vine until May. Even so the wine may not turn out to be heavy and dark.

Colin Preece won many an award with his big soft reds. To gain the right effect he sometimes blended in with the

Great Western wine, some of the weighty flavorous wine
of his company's winery at Rutherglen. These were never
my favourite wines. Each to his own taste as the French
say. If Seppelt's have a market for this type of wine they
should certainly do everything in their power to maintain
it. Blended wines have a place in our wine structure and can
certainly rate among our great wines, but in my ideal
scheme of wine hierarchy, I believe that only straight
unblended wines can ever be entitled to be appellation
'Outstanding'.

In 1964, I wrote a passage on a straight Great Western
red made by Best's in 1961. Reading it over, I realize that
it depicts my perfect Great Western red:

If ever you have a half hour to spend in silent and pensive
contemplation of a wine take this Great Western red. Pour a little
into a tulip shaped glass and sit the glass on a white table cloth.
If it is evening, switch on your brightest lights. The wine is the
purest red. Look at it from every angle. With the light shining
directly through it, it is pigeon's blood. The reflected rays from
the white cloth produce deep ruby. Gaze at it from the top and
you will see the faintest pink on the edges, the deepest rose in the
middle. This is an exciting chain of colour images producing
the most satisfying pleasure in that part of the mind which is
perceptive of sensed beauty.

Cup one hand around the bowl of the glass and place the palm
of the other over the lip, capturing and compressing the odiferous
vapours so they rise from the body warmed wine. Then allow
the olfactory senses to enjoy their share of pleasure. These are
the sensory pleasures of the fields – wild flowers and mown
grass, the perfume of headed wheat and reaped oats. One by one
the aromas rise and strike the sense of smell, each with a deep
and different impact.

Sip the wine which by now should be of body temperature.
Allow it to roll slowly around the tongue. You will notice it
biting and roughening the surface. It creeps around the inside
surfaces of the lips and pulls at them. Then it reaches the middle
of the tongue and its flavour begins to seep into the palate as
though this were blotting paper. The liquid is heated more
rapidly and the released esters rise to the sensory organs at the
top of the palate. They are similar to the odours arising from a
chest of Ceylonese tea.

Here in the middle of the palate the flavour is intense, over-laden with ripe apples and peaches and brazil nuts. There are other essences and perfumes too, all of which produce a delicate effect, a light touch which stimulates the palate and delights the heart.

The wine rises over the hill of the tongue and departs leaving a thin layer of flavours in its trail which is quite different from the first more definite taste. It leaves odiferous vapours and a tactual sensation of drawn and puckered surfaces as though the wine had spread generously its flowers and scent but had erased all other flavours as it passed.

Perhaps I would not be quite so garrulous today.

White wines from Great Western are a different pro-position to the red. I have never found a Great Western white which did not completely lose its character when blended with a wine outside the area. As straight wines they are superb, comparing favourably (if well made) with the high quality wines of Mersault. The older they are (in bottle) the better.

The Seppelt organization handle their whites perfectly. Their technical men are highly skilled, their equipment is top class and there is every reason to believe that we shall see an ever-increasing quantity of outstanding district whites from this company as the years go by. Seppelt's are far too wise, however, to pin their hopes and future to this one frail area. Their vineyards at Drumborg and Keppoch are already feeding the winery with champagne material. They are planting only the most suitable varieties at Great Western and any new plantings are always made cautiously with one eye on the frost pattern and history of the paddock being planted. There is a future for Great Western wines of the still variety but only, I am afraid, from specially chosen vineyards where the lie and aspect minimizes the risk of frost, and there are not many paddocks with suitable soil which conform to those limited conditions. Great Western straight wines will always be in short supply, therefore, and will always be expensive. Who knows? A tiny patch of frost-free ground in this area may one day be as valuable as a city block.

The climate of Great Western and the surrounding district is such that, on a very general basis, one could assume that wines of quality up to the standard of Bordeaux, the Rhone Valley and the Côte d'Or would be possible.

Peter Weste of Seppelt's Great Western winery, holds that the red wines of the district are similar to those of the Rhone Valley and I agree with him. Few people outside France realize that Hermitage from the Rhone is regarded as equal to the best of Bordeaux and Burgundy.

The average mean temperature of the hottest month of this district is 21 °C which is approximately the same as that of the other classic wine districts of the world. The pattern of ripening, and hence of harvesting, is once again similar to that of the great wine districts of the world. Picking of early ripening varieties, such as pinot noir begins early in the first month of autumn. That of middle ripening varieties like shiraz begins at the end of the first month and into the second month. If they are picked at the end of the second month these varieties are too ripe and have lost too much acid.

Both Bordeaux and the Côte d'Or areas of France have adopted the modern practice of picking as soon as the grape is ripe with emphasis on retaining as much acid in the grape as possible. Even a little early picking is preferable to leaving the fruit on the vine too long. Seppelt's and Best's are well aware of these modern methods and hence attention to harvesting at the right time is, to them, of prime importance.

Rainfall at Great Western is not sufficient for the development of healthy vines. Grape growers in the area will have to develop a system of drip irrigation. Unfortunately the underground natural storage reservoirs are too salty for this purpose but dams, tanks and the Concongella Creek are all used to supply such systems. Winter rainfall is sufficient to create a satisfactory reserve of water for late spring and early summer.

The height above sea level at Great Western varies roughly between 290 metres and 365 metres. This and the latitude, 37° south, gives the cool temperatures for the desired slow ripening of the fruit and the retention of acid.

Around the hamlet itself, there are about 260 hectares of vineyard land which can be developed economically.

The flats along the Concongella Creek have good soil and some of the higher regions around the Great Western winery possess a heavy loam. With clonal selection and drip irrigation, it should be possible to crop 4·06 tonnes to half a hectare of varieties such as shiraz, chasselas and Irvine's white. Cabernet, according to Peter Weste, needs more water than the district can supply.

Most of the remaining soil of this small area is badly leached podsol and completely uneconomic as vineyard land. It is important for the reputation of Great Western that clonal selection of vines for new plantings is based more on quality factors than size of crops. Hence clones are chosen because of the weight of the bunches and the baume reading at picking time.

Seppelt's, along with so many other quality winemakers, rely on the judgement of men like Peter Weste to determine the date of harvesting rather than baume/acid ratios. Peter thinks that the time must come when scientific readings will replace the chewing of the grapes but these readings will be based on recordings of sugar and acid at the time of picking for any particular vineyard section as already determined by the experts using the tasting method.

In quality areas, the retention of acid in the ripe grape is considered far more important than any other factor. A grape therefore may have a sugar content of 10 or 12 baume without causing the winemaker to do anything but nod his head; but if his acid drops below 6 grams per litre he becomes concerned. In small vineyards, where picking can be completed within a few days, as is the case at Great Western, exactly desirable acid content can be achieved.

Because of frost damage and cool weather, Great Western reds are sometimes a little light in colour. The best of them have a Japanese plum hue. The nose is clean and perfumed giving the impression of high quality. There is good clean acid on the palate, plentiful flavour especially on the middle palate. The palate is left clean and the finish is firm and astringent. They respond well to a little ageing in good casks which have not held many previous wines. Too much oak or poor oak spoils them. Without any question they are among the best wines of Australia and can compete well with the best wines of the world.

There remains the famous **Great Western Champagne** of Seppelt's. There has been a manifold increase in the production of this fine sparkling wine over the last ten years, because of larger buildings, more plant, more technicians and the technique known as the 'transfer method'. One would expect that quality would have deteriorated. My only complaint is that the more popular and lower priced line **Imperial Reserve**, lacks that typically French champagne flavour which is apparent in the line, **Vintage Brut**.

Two factors obviously rule in this area. First, only top quality district white grapes are used in the Vintage Brut and, secondly, it is aged longer on the lees in bottle to allow the 'yeast autolysis' flavour to develop more satisfactorily.

Seppelt's are faced with the problem of how to use their top grade Great Western material, both red and white. It is necessary for them to maintain a high standard of quality in all the wines they blend, age and bottle at Great Western. For this purpose, although wines and grapes come into the winery from other areas, a certain amount of Great Western wine must be blended into their Imperial Reserve Champagne, their Sparkling Burgundy, their Chalambar, Moyston, Arawatta, Rhymney and Melita wines. A small amount can be reserved for marketing as Great Western 'straight' wines but it cannot be and never will be a very large quantity.

Seppelt's can develop about 240 hectares economically at Great Western. The very best they can expect to crop is four tonnes to 0·4 hectare. In years of frost they are certain to lose a percentage of the crops grown on the river flats. This would give them perhaps a maximum in full production of 1364 kl a year. This has to be blended to produce several million bottles of champagne and millions of bottles of the table wines mentioned above. Even granted a most generous gesture to wine lovers, the straight Great Western wines are going to be very few.

Best's have twenty or so hectares of vines but situated, as they are, on the low lying flats, their losses by frost are likely to be heavy and frequent.

One must not despair, however. Seppelt's do have several other quality areas which will help eke out Great Western sources for blending wine. Keppoch, Drumborg, Barooga and Rutherglen have given hope that much first quality material will be available.

In addition, quite a number of grape growers in nearby surrounding districts will be supplying their fruit to both wineries. **Des McRae** and his two sons, Greg and Michael, have a magnificent property of nearly 16 hectares at Ararat situated on a frost free patch of hillside with glorious red volcanic loam and plenty of water. The **Dalkin** family, on the tallest hill only a few kilometres away from Great Western, have planted 8 hectares of vines on dark chocolate loam and gravel.

Several large properties are planted near Avoca in frost free areas and it appears that all of them except Chateau Remy will wish to market their grapes rather than invest capital in building and equipping a winery.

These grapes, no doubt, will be made into wine and sold by both Seppelt's and Best's as 'Great Western District' wines. I have already tasted straight Avoca wines made by **Chateau Remy** and have assessed them as top quality. The future, therefore, is not as gloomy for wine lovers as it could be.

Yet I hope that we shall see top quality wines made from grapes grown at Great Western itself, especially selected for their distinction above all others, carefully nurtured, aged in good wood and carefully bottled, bearing a label which clearly indicates their exact origin. Such a wine may be one I tasted with Peter Weste in 1971. It would be labelled

Bin 113/68 Great Western Hermitage 1968. My notes say,
'The colour is dense, heavy crimson. The nose is clean and
perfumed. The middle palate is full, fruity, rich and
pleasant. A big wine with a great deal of wood character
which should soften. A classic wine.' What about the cost
of these wines? Considering the paucity of material which
will be available for these special high class binnings and
the care that will be required to prepare them, I cannot see
them selling under three dollars a bottle.

I should imagine that they could be held in oak hogs-
heads of 22·7 kl capacity. They will have to be given special
devoted attention so that at least one highly trained winemaker will be spending his time with them. The comparative
costs can be seen. A batch of 455 kl of wine can be cared for
quite well by the part time supervision of a winemaker and
a few winery workers. Three lots of 22·7 kl each could
take a similar highly paid winemaker and as many workers.
The vigneron has gone to particular trouble to watch the
growing and maturing of the grapes and their harvesting.
The winery manager spends a great deal of time inspecting
the special wines and consulting with the vigneron, the
wine chemist and the winemaker; and so the long and
costly process of special attention multiplies in every
direction.

In any field there is an astronomical cost difference in
producing a good quality article and a perfect one. It will
be interesting, therefore, to see what Seppelt's and Best's
will want for these top grade special selections. My guess
is that it will be three times as much as for the best wines
from their other areas.

Drumborg perhaps is the most surprising of the new
districts. It is very close to Portland and therefore much
further south than Coonawarra or even Geelong. One is
tempted to conjecture that it may be too cold for grape
growing and that there will be several years in a cycle when
the grapes will not ripen at all. However, besides Seppelt's
venture in this area several other enterprising people have
entered the field here. Certainly the soil is most promising,

being of a volcanic nature with traces of lime and ironstone. It is very friable, easy to work and absorbs moisture readily. The locals say that the weather does not frighten them because a high ridge protects them from the cold westerlies which blow in from the sea.

Seppelt's are planting their Drumborg property with grape varieties which are most suitable for making their champagne. They have a variety which seems to be theirs alone, the 'Irvine's white', which is so similar to the pinot blanc that for many years it was thought to be such.

Goulburn Valley

In the last ten years there has been a gradually emerging picture of the Goulburn Valley as a homogeneous viti-cultural area separate in character from the nearby north-east Victorian region and embracing only slight climatic differences to influence different flavours in wines grown in a comparatively small area of the Valley.

The grapes are grown in the region where the river has left behind the rolling hills and the sharper valleys of the Great Dividing Range. The present areas of existing vines and of those now being planted out, are in the flat part of the valley where, in the past, the river tended to meander and flood its banks, depositing mud and silt and forming billabongs. The creation of the Eildon Reservoir has stopped such destruction. The sandy loam flats, with sometimes a clay loam subsoil, are highly suitable for fruit growing and hence also for the grape.

At present grapes are grown at Seymour, Tahbilk and Shepparton. The closer we approach the ranges, the more similar is the climate to the classic regions of the world. The further north we travel the hotter the summers, the greater the heat summation and the more quickly the grape matures.

The new project of Ross and Marigold Shelmerdine at **Mitchelton** near Tahbilk will certainly be just as successful as Chateau Tahbilk itself. With improved methods and more up-to-date equipment and methods the existing vineyards of **Darveniza** and **Gravina** should be constant producers of high quality wine. Since these latter wineries use a great deal of material from vineyards in the Murray Valley it would be wise for them to state clearly on their labels the origin of the grapes which made the wine. Because of their much higher quality, straight Goulburn Valley wines will fetch a much higher price than those made from vines grown in the hot central regions of the Murray Valley.

The project begun by **Fitzpatrick Bros** at Seymour should be just as successful. Of course, until the wine is made no one knows how good or bad it will be but all the indications are that it will be top quality. Once again the temptation to market wines under a label without indicating the true origin of the grape material will have to be resisted. Let us hope that all the Goulburn Valley makers will be jealous of the reputation of this fertile section of vineyard country.

When one looks at the Goulburn Valley to determine whether it is or is not a high quality area, one is forced to depend solely on the reputation of Chateau Tahbilk and to a lesser extent on that of Darveniza's Excelsior Winery at Mooroopna. When the latter winery is mentioned it should be remembered that, before the turn of the century, its wines won hundreds of European awards against competition from the rest of the winemaking world.

In general Goulburn Valley wines exhibit the ripe berry flavour of the wines of the Rutherglen area, but are not nearly so fully flavoured, nor do they have the tendency to the 'blackberry jam' taste that so characterizes these latter wines.

CHATEAU TAHBILK

Chateau Tahbilk, situated in the ideal position in the Goulburn Valley in central Victoria, has an average mean summer temperature comparable to high quality vineyard areas in other parts of the world; its number of sun hours during the ripening period is comparable to Great Western; vintaging is in middle autumn which is close enough to being ideal. The soil is fertile and suited to the vine. Rainfall is usually sufficient but if it fails in some years the matter is irrelevant as supplementary watering can be supplied by pumps drawing supplies from the river.

Tahbilk has not built up the same reputation as the Hunter Valley or Coonawarra areas and this is probably mainly because of the size of the vineyard area. There seems to be an unconscious belief that if a vineyard is capable of producing top quality wines, it should be surrounded by vineyards. The fact that it is not would seem to indicate that the area is unsuccessful in this respect. Of course, the reasoning is quite false. The history of wine in Australia shows quite clearly that dry wine areas survived the difficult economic times, when practically no table wines were consumed in Australia and only the very heavy types were exported, because of the fantastic belief of the owners that one day demand would grow. Courage and perseverance alone were not enough. Such forward-looking men had to support themselves by other primary industries such as farming and grazing. This is exactly what the Purbrick family did.

Now that other vineyard ventures have been begun very close to Chateau Tahbilk in the Goulburn Valley, the question about the ranking of Chateau Tahbilk wines is being posed more seriously. There have been those who have never doubted the superiority of the wines. A small group of Melbourne connoisseurs including Tom Seabrook, de Castella, David Sutherland Smith and Bill Nairn considered them outstanding long before the name became generally well known. The great Maurice O'Shea was impressed with the potentiality of the area.

The Show record of Chateau Tahbilk has not been remarkable. It has picked up gold, silver and bronze awards over the years but these could never create the gong crashing effect enjoyed by the larger companies with huge production and almost unlimited resources. Yet Tahbilk has enjoyed sufficient reputation over the years to place its reds in the 'great' classification. Perhaps the number of outstanding wines were fewer in earlier years than that of other quality areas. Perhaps many of the wines have been too heavy in body and tended to be too full and over rich in the typical 'old fashioned' Australian red style, in order to qualify as world class.

Still, I can remember three reds which were equivalent to the best I have tasted in Australia. The first was the **1938 Bin 5X** which was acclaimed by wine men in Melbourne and Sydney just after the war. It was a big wine but its flavour, tannin finish and perfect balance placed it in world class. The second was the **1944** bottled by **Maurice O'Shea**. It also was a big wine and threw a tremendous deposit. For some reason many wine men picked it as a Hunter Valley wine. The third was the **1948**, a red in many ways almost a replica of the 5X but a little lighter in style. In the sixties **Eric Purbrick** made a succession of perfect wines beginning with the **1961**. Without question the straight cabernet sauvignon has been the best of these and it seems probable that this is the grape variety most suited to the area. The future may prove otherwise and, at all events, I am very fond of his lighter style straight shiraz reds. Almost every year now sees a great Purbrick red on the market and in classifying his Cabernet Sauvignon as 'very great' I am looking at these recent vintages made in the modern wine idiom rather than those of many years ago.

In the table on page 1 I have decided the Goulburn Valley into 'Central' and 'Northern'. Chateau Tahbilk in the Central area produces wines lighter than those of say, Darveniza, further north. The greater heat of the northern Goulburn Valley seems likely to produce heavier wines than those of Tahbilk and a distinction is therefore necessary. Certainly the wines of Darveniza, although excellent, are very heavy and have a flavour which is not found in the Tahbilk wines.

North-east Victoria

Barossa Valley winemakers face the problem of changing the image of the area from that of a producer of fortified wine to that of a district capable of producing high quality table wine. A similar problem is faced by the vignerons of north-east Victoria. But the difficulty in the latter area is more one of the philosophy of the winemaker than one of actual viniculture. Even today some advertisements ask, 'Do you remember the big soft gusty wines of north-east Victoria?' There is a nostalgia for these so called big fat red wines. Whether this type of red can be described as 'typical' of and 'peculiar' to the region is doubtful. McLaren Vale, the Barossa Valley and Swan Valley also make big fat reds; but not every year, nor by every winemaker. It is usually a question of whether or not the areas experience a long hot summer and whether the winemaker wants to make that kind of wine.

Similarly the north-east is renowned for its soft ports and liqueur muscats. In former times it was also famed for its huge cask-aged sherries but of latter years its prowess in this direction has lost its appeal. Few people want old full bodied sherries nowadays.

The metamorphosis of Rutherglen from a producer of fortified wines to that of one making high quality table wines has been hampered to a great extent by the shortage of wine in the last eight years. Large sales at the cellar door to streams of passing tourists has not helped to create that *élan* vital necessary to produce masterpieces. Hence masterpieces from the north-east have not been seen in recent years.

No question can be raised regarding the quality of the fortified wines since the whole wine world recognizes the superior place occupied in the industry by the ports and muscats of Morris, Sutherland Smith, Chambers and Bailey.

Although pleasant, easy to drink, comforting and warming in winter, the old style, high alcohol dark red wines of this corner of Victoria will never rank as world quality wines. Yet it cannot be denied that the area has the potential to produce great red and white table wines. The frequent flashes of brilliance seen in a **Booth's** or a **Brown's**, the occasional high quality white from **Morris** and the highly scientific methods of **George Sutherland Smith Junior** in making table wine leave little room for doubt that in the future the star of the north-east will shine again, and then upon those who love unfortified wine.

There are other problems. Not every oenologist would be happy with the climate of Rutherglen. It has extended hot summers which result in a heat summation and a total of sun hours far beyond the ideal. There are many vine diseases in the area which have to be overcome. There are no slopes to relieve the flat topography of the area and thus the chance of lessening the afternoon heat and light by the shadow of a hill does not exist. Naturally this cannot be said of the Booths and Baileys at Taminick nor of the Browns at Everton.

There is, I am sure, a fairly wide margin in the range of temperature of areas where grapes are grown, in which the winemaker can use his skill to counter nature. The genius in these regions will make superb wines. The plodder will produce no better than can be expected from the climate. So it will be in the north-east of Victoria.

MILAWA

North-east Victoria presents a good example of a small wine-growing area the product of which is so uneven in quality that it retains its title as a compact wine district only because it is so geographically. It adds a tiny piece of evidence to the theory that there is no single area in the world which can claim that it can produce, throughout its length and breadth, top quality wines. One side of a hill in the Rhine Valley can consistently produce superb white wines; the other side will consistently bring forth something only a little better than vinegar.

North-east Victoria clearly conforms to such a pattern. Climate, aspect, hills and valleys are obviously major elements in creating quality differences between various vineyards in the same region.

In addition, but just as important, is the difference in

quality of the winemakers themselves. In his suggested revision of the Bordeaux Classification of 1855, Alexis Lichine says: 'The fact that a great soil, given proper management, will produce great wines, was taken into account; certain vineyards have not been downgraded as much as their present management warrants, because the soil is intact and, under new management, these vineyards will rise again. A classification should not be planned for a shorter span than 25 years or half a century'. The conclusion which may be drawn even further from this statement is that there may be in odd places of the world some existing vineyards, not now accepted as great, which, given correct management, can make outstanding wine.

I believe that the vineyard of **Brown Brothers**, of Milawa in north-east Victoria, may be an excellent example of this situation. It has taken John Brown twenty-five years to show that he can produce very great Australian wine.

I did not believe that John Brown's wines of the late forties and fifties were great wines. In my opinion their touch of quality was rare, and, when it occurred, the wine did not retain it for many years. I believe that the wine John Brown is making today can occasionally reach great heights, and will last much longer.

In conducting an agricultural or horticultural property it may take many years before the land can produce as the owner desires. But if the agriculturalist is intelligent, dedicated, persevering and holds to his ideas, the property will eventually commence to produce in the desired way. I believe, this was the problem and history of John Brown of Milawa.

His sons are undoubtedly parts of his winemaking machine – four highly intelligent and vigorous young men who are as dedicated as their father.

The Brown family has its own wine philosophy, and, therefore, produces highly distinctive wines. They believe in studying and applying the most modern methods of viticulture and winemaking, in addition to adhering to the well-proved methods of the past. Hence in their winery is the machinery part of modern winemaking – the fluted crusher, the Boucher press, the centrifuge, the cold fermenters, the stainless steel and the new oak.

Will the Brown philosophy produce world-class Australian wines? No part of north-east Victoria has so far won the acclaim of Coonawarra or Hunter Valley. John Brown and his sons make beautiful wines of great character. Their whites are in the modern wine idiom of Germany and Alsace. Their reds are soft, rich and exciting like the best wines of Piedmont. Irrespective of whether they rival these wines on their particular standards, they have won a place among Australia's great wines.

New Areas
GEELONG
Every day stories come pouring into my office of new vineyards being planted in areas which once were famed for the quality of their wines, but which have been out of production for at least sixty years.

Waurn Ponds is one such district. This little hamlet is a few miles out of Geelong on the Colac road. In the latter part of last century Geelong district wines, both dry white and dry red, were renowned for their fineness. It is remarkable to find in old records how often they won medals and awards in the great exhibitions which were held in Australia around about this time and even in the international exhibitions which were held in England and Europe. It seems that a strikingly bright burst of enthusiasm has broken out among the local landowners at Waurn Ponds. Grape varieties of the classical styles have been planted by many of them and grape growing and wine production has become one of the main topics of conversation around Geelong.

MOORABOOL
Here at their vineyard, Idyll, a few miles out of Geelong on the Anakie road, Daryl and Nini Sefton have established a plot of vines of about a hectare in size. It produced its first wine in 1972. It gives promise that their wines in the future will be of extremely high quality.

BENDIGO

In 1873, at a Viennese exhibition of the wines of the world, it is reported that first prize was given to an Australian red wine made at Bendigo. According to the story received in Australia the judges walked out on the grounds that a French red had been substituted for the Australian wine. In 1875 phylloxera struck Bendigo and under a Victorian statute all vines in the area were uprooted and the wines made there were salted. No further attempt was made to grow vines in the Bendigo area until in 1969 young **Stuart Anderson** purchased 81 hectares of land at Marong, just outside the city and began planting 8 hectares with shiraz and cabernet. In 1970 he planted experimental plots with merlot, pinot noir, traminer, chardonnay, and three different clones of rhine riesling. This vineyard is, in my opinion, the beginning of a great revival of wine growing in the Bendigo area.

Stuart Anderson's aim is to produce relatively small quantities of top quality dry whites and reds with a district character. I feel sure that soon many people will follow his example. It is almost certain that within the next fifty years Bendigo will become an important viticultural centre. Stuart has had only three vintages, both being necessarily very small. It is difficult to judge, therefore, what the pattern of the wines of the area will be like. Based on my tastings of the 1972 and 1973 reds of Stuart Anderson alone, I would say that in the Marong Shire we have another classical area comparing in quality with Great Western and hence likely to produce some of the outstanding dry reds of Australia.

Unfortunately, Stuart has no climatic data with which to compare his area with other great areas of the world. He thinks that the number of day degrees would be 2900 to 3000. This compares with 2632 at Bordeaux. According to the map produced by J. A. Prescott of the Wine Research Institute, Bendigo would have a mean temperature in the warmest month of 68°F (20°C) – much the same as Bordeaux. Heat summation is found by multiplying the number of days with temperatures of over 50°F (10°C) by the number of degrees over 10. This gives the number of day degrees. The period examined is that from the beginning of the growth of the vine after dormancy to the time of vintage.

Stuart claims that there is plenty of cloud cover in the summer months, a factor which would create a lesser number of sun hours and tend to dampen the effect of the long hot summers which are typical of inland areas of Victoria north of the dividing range. Rainfall of the area is only 571·5 mm. Frost is a springtime hazard. The soil is a sandy loam over clay and gravel from slate and shale parent rock. The vine has to struggle, therefore, against some deficiencies of nature. Stuart says that this is the pattern of classic wines – the fact that they have to produce wine under marginal conditions. I would back his confidence.

Working on the only two vintages he has to show, we can form some judgement on the wines by observing that the grapes were picked at 13° Baume at an acid content of 7·5 grams per litre. With so much acid at so high a sugar content, the possibility of obtaining fresh vigorous reds is most likely. This is supported by my tasting of the wines. The 1973 shiraz, being a free run with some pressings added, with about six weeks in new American oak elicited the following comments: 'opaque violet/heliotrope colour with a spicy floral nose. The palate indicated the presence of a great deal of grape tannin in addition to the oak tannin, with a plentiful flavour, clean and penetrating. The centre palate showed the same "non-sugar" sweetness as experienced in a top Bordeaux, with absolutely different flavour characteristics such as nutmeg and allspice. The grape comes through with a berry taste. It should live a long time.'

The 1973 cabernet has the same dense violet colour, a bouquet carrying glorious spice, sweetish and faintly floral, faintly cinnamon. On the palate it is finely textured with a strong flavour of oak and a great tannin grip. The centre palate shows plentiful flavour, not rich but penetrating. The finish is extremely clean and the flavours linger on. It is an outstanding wine.

7 New South Wales

The Hunter Valley and Surrounding Areas

In many ways the viticultural area of the Hunter Valley is an enigma. To begin with, it does not seem to fit into any of the patterns typical of the classic wine areas of the world. Secondly it is far closer to the equator than an academic oenologist would think wise. Thirdly, harvesting is at the peak of the summer when the probability of oxidation of juices and must is at its greatest and bacteria, moulds and wild yeasts are most rampant. Finally, the ripening curve of the grape is far too sharp for a classified area.

Yet it cannot be denied that the Hunter produces first class wines. This might not be so obvious to the Frenchman or Englishman who has conditioned his palate to the top quality reds and whites of Bordeaux and Bourgogne. I think it might be more easily recognized by the relatively unbiased American, Japanese or Canadian. I qualify this statement, however, by stating my personal opinion that very few Hunter wineries make top grade vintages very often and certainly not in many successive years. Furthermore, I suggest that the number of top grade red wines are rare for a reputedly top grade red area; and ultimately the reputation of the Hunter rests almost entirely on the consistently high quality of its white wines.

It is not my object to solve the enigma of the Hunter; but only to discuss the various factors which make it so.

The apparent enigma may be analyzed by looking first at the *a priori* judgement made immediately the climatic picture of the Hunter is examined and secondly by a study of the history of Hunter wines' uneven quality over the past thirty years.

I hope to show that (a) the Hunter Valley unquestionably produces top quality wines, both red and white; (b) these wines appear sporadically. In other words the general run of Hunter wines is somewhat of the secondary order from that expected of an area showing its climatic data; only in odd years or in an odd run of years are these top quality wines produced; (c) white wines and red wines do not often show the same top quality factors in the same year; (d) generally white wines show top quality factors more frequently than red; and (e) the possible reason for these diverse results is the extremely diverse behaviour of weather in the Hunter Valley.

There was a period in my wine life when I was puzzled by the excessive number of accolades accorded Hunter wines. It is only in recent years that I have come to see that my judgement of their quality was clouded by the many average wines from the district that came to my tasting rooms in the years from 1945 to 1960. The really great Hunters of recent years have given me a far deeper appreciation of the quality of the region.

Where do the Hunter wines fit in among the great wines of the world? My conclusion is that they do not conform to the characteristics of any other region; that some of them are great wines in their own right, different from any other, similar in quality to the great wines of Europe but distinctive in flavour.

The inference, or even the direct statement, that a Hunter white is like a French chablis is beyond my comprehension. I have never tasted the similarity and the use of the word 'chablis' in the context is personally abhorrent. I can understand why the French wine man cannot bear the use of the term for any wine but that which comes from the tiny area of Chablis in France. In my gustatory experience, in a good year when their distinctive taste factors are obvious, well-made Hunter Valley wines do strike a common chord with well-made French wines from quality areas. A top grade Hunter white is nothing like a German, an Alsatian, an Italian or an Austrian white but it has a general recognizable affinity with white wines from Bordeaux or Burgundy. Similarly, a top Hunter red has a taste relationship with most good red wines from France whether they come from Bordeaux, the Rhone Valley or the Midi.

To align a Hunter red wine with a red wine from the Côte d'Or is so patently off beam that I doubt if any responsible wine man would dare to use the comparison today. A French Côte d'Or burgundy is made from pinot noir grapes. This factor alone makes it very different from Hunter Valley reds which are mostly made from shiraz. The pinot noir produces a fairly light pinkish wine. Over a number of years this darkens and it becomes similar in colour to red wines made from grapes with more pigment; but, even so, the difference in colour is fairly easily detected.

Even Burgundy wines made from the gamay grape, which is a different strain of the pinot noir, have a light crimson colour very different from the colour of a cabernet or shiraz. The smell and taste of pinot noir or gamay wine is very distinctive. Hence, even apart from district characteristics, the red wines from the Hunter are very different to those of Burgundy. I can accept the use of the word 'burgundy' as meaning a soft, smooth, red wine but, if the implication in the use of the term is that an Australian wine has taste similarities to that of a French burgundy, then my mind is not with the speaker.

The two most articulate speakers and lucid writers on Hunter wines are Len Evans and Max Lake. Len's acute judgement and the fact that he has obviously tasted Hunter wines much older than those of the sixties, makes his assessment of the quality of various vintages and winemakers very accurate. Max has a distinct bias towards Hunter wines and this tends to cause him to praise wines of lesser years far more than they deserve. On the other hand, his palate is finely attuned and his memory is good; he has a keen intellect and an intensive mind. His assessment, therefore, of Hunter wines is most valuable. Although I have centred my articles on my own experiences and opinions of the Hunter, much of what I have to say is based on the dissertations of these two men.

Max Lake begins the preface to his book, *Hunter Winemakers*, with the following quotation from St Augustine: 'The truth is neither mine, nor his, nor another's; but belongs to us all whom Thou callest to partake of it; warning us terribly, not to account it private to ourselves, lest we be deprived of it'. Perhaps it is surprising that an agnostic, such as Max, should quote St Augustine. In this instance, Max is relating the quotation to the wines and winemakers of the Hunter, so it might be apposite to add that not everyone who thinks he knows Hunter wine has all of the truth. All of us have some of it. If we could piece together everything each of us knows a totally different picture of Hunter wines would emerge. There can be no doubt that Max Lake is the great thinker, the great genius of the Hunter. Maurice O'Shea was, in my opinion, 'the old fox', the brilliant winemaker, the innovator, the great adaptor. Max Lake is the scientist-philosopher.

I have endeavoured to look at all Hunter wines on a world wide level. If I have been critical it is because I wish Australians not to be thought of as chauvinistic about their wines, insular, provincial and biased. We have had too much criticism in the past of our sensitivity to criticism. I hope at a future time to limn the great picture of glory which I feel is in store for this centre of winemaking.

It would not be difficult to prove that the Hunter Valley produces top quality wines. Those of us who have sat around wine tables every week for more than twenty years and tasted masked wines of all countries, discussed them with the best judges of wine, with the top wine men from overseas, and listened well to learned opinions, will know beyond doubt that some Hunters compare favourably with the best wines from any country. There is no need, therefore, to produce instances and examples, nor to indicate the truth of the proposition except to state that we who have seen and listened know that it is true.

The mean summer temperature of the valley is 24°C (75°F). That of classical areas such as Bordeaux and Burgundy is 20°C (68°F). Cessnock (near Pokolbin, centre of the Lower Hunter), with a latitude of 33°S, experiences an average yearly heat summation of 4330 degree days. Burgundy, with a latitude of 47°N, experiences 2327 day degrees, and Bordeaux (latitude 45°N) experiences 2632 day degrees. Cessnock in fact has a higher heat summation than Griffith with 4170 degree days. It is apparent immediately that, to produce top quality wine under these conditions, extraordinary techniques in making must be adopted. More than average attention must be given to preventing oxidation of juice and the newly made wine. Temperatures of rooms where the wine is aged must be kept at reasonable levels during the summer.

It is important to comprehend that, more significant probably than temperature in the production of quality wine, is the number of sunshine hours experienced by a vineyard. Sunshine or light is the catalyst which causes photosynthesis, the chemical concatenation whereby carbon, oxygen and hydrogen are converted into sugar which eventually finds itself in the grape berry. If we compare the sunlight hours of the viticultural areas mentioned above, we find a pattern quite different to that of day degrees. Bordeaux has 237; Burgundy 250, and Cessnock 249. Griffith has 327.

Vintaging commences in Bordeaux and Burgundy in September, the first month of autumn. It begins in the Hunter in early February, or the third month of summer. All this seems to indicate that the higher temperatures in the Hunter, rather than the number of light hours, hasten ripening of the crop. In any event, the grape variety to a great extent determines the time of ripening rather than the temperature for any particular area. It appears that the saving factor in the Hunter is the relatively small number of sunlight hours.

Yet it is patently clear that grapes picked in autumn give

the winemaker an advantage over the maker who is crushing grapes picked in the middle of summer. It does not take an expert to realize that oxidation of juices must take place far more rapidly on hot days, that bacteria develop more easily and that hotter fermentations are more likely to occur unless extensive refrigeration is used. If care is not taken, the winemaker can finish up with a brownish coloured red wine, sometimes burnt or looking like stewed plums.

In spite of all this, the best red wines of the Hunter have undoubtedly been produced in the hot dry years.

As in many other wine areas of Australia the wines of the Hunter can be very ordinary. Very often the reds are brown rather than crimson and the oxidation of colour is often reflected in the oxidation of other components in the wine. More often than not they taste slightly coarse or earthy. The chief flavour characteristic of the reds, and that by which I recognize them most easily, is that of tar, not altogether unpleasant, but, to my mind, not altogether enjoyable. Very often the whites are flat and uninteresting with a taste which reminds me of very dry straw sweltering in the hot noon-day sun. Once again this is not an unpleasant flavour, but, to me, it is not interesting.

These are the ordinary wines. There are a great number of ordinary wines, too, produced around Bordeaux and Beaune, but they never appear under a well known label. In view of the climatic data I have given above it is not surprising that ordinary wines should occur in the Hunter more often than not.

Since, however, heat summation and number of daylight hours are not universal factors in any but very flat areas such as Griffith, it follows that the micro-climates of Pokolbin-Rothbury could result in conditions which will produce top quality wines at one vineyard and poor at another in the same year. The vineyards of Pokolbin-Rothbury are planted on hillsides. The protection from the hot afternoon sun afforded by the shadow of a hill or the slope of the land must inevitably affect the quality of the wine.

A wet summer usually means a lower mean temperature. It certainly results in a lesser number of sunlight hours. It is interesting to note Max Lake's comments on these factors. In *Hunter Winemakers* he says: 'Assessment of the effect of weather on a Hunter vintage is difficult. The grapes ripen to vintage point from the end of January to the end of March . . . Hail or rain can come early or late and great wines may be made in bad weather years, depending on whether or not they have missed the bad weather'. He adds, 'What are the ideal conditions for the production of top wine? Good winter rain for the subsoil, and some rain at spring flowering to set the fruit evenly, followed by a fairly dry summer with cool evenings and an occasional shower to fill out the berries before vintage'. That is a definition of ideal conditions which would apply anywhere in the world. Such a set of conditions is rare in the Hunter.

In the years **1937 to 1949 Maurice O'Shea** and **Lindeman's** marketed a series of superb red and white wines which are a by-word in Australia to this day. Since both these firms were large buyers of wines from the other makers in the area and used the top wines of these other makers as components in their best binnings, it appears that the whole of the Hunter in those years produced world quality top wines. In **1952** O'Shea made the glorious **Stephen Hermitage**. **Tulloch's** produced a cracker red and **Drayton's** and **Phillip's** whites marketed by Leo Buring were incredibly good. Although information about earlier vintages is scarce we do know that **O'Shea** made some great reds in **1933** and **1935** and the famous **Caldwell** red of **1933** was quite easily as good as any French wine we had seen in Australia during that era.

It is significant perhaps that from the turn of the century to the mid 1940s, annual rainfall was generally less than average. This means, of course, that the sunshine was greater and the summers were hotter. The pattern of rainfall in the Valley shows that the summer months have the highest average rainfalls. It can happen, naturally, that sudden summer storms can result in torrential rain over a very short period which can even cause severe flooding, although the remainder of the summer is hot and dry. This seems to have happened in the flood years of 1949 and 1951. Usually, however, the rain in a wet year persists during the summer, causing a cloud cover with loss of sun hours and lowering of temperatures. Rainfall from 1950 to the early 1960s was consistently higher than average, and I think that this factor reflects itself in the quality of the reds of those years. I cannot remember tasting any Hunter red made after 1952 and up to 1963 which I considered to come up to any of the Lindeman's or O'Shea's of the previous decade. Most of the reds were soft, easy to drink and pleasant, but were by no means great.

There was a severe drought from July 1964 to early 1967 and some of the reds of that period were among the best ever made, with 1965 producing superlative wines from every vineyard. This does seem to me to indicate that only in odd years or in an odd run of years do we see top quality Hunters.

On the other hand, bad weather and cool summers, while undoubtedly creating conditions which produce mediocre reds, seem to produce first class whites.

During the period of the regal reds of the 1940s, I cannot remember drinking any white wines, whether made by O'Shea or Lindeman's, which set me to thinking that they were on a level with the great wines of the world. Yet, right throughout the 1950s I was enthralled with the lovely rich, soft whites made by Phillip's, Drayton's, Tulloch's and Lindeman's. There was scarcely a year in that decade when one or another of these firms did not produce a great white.

Penfold's brought out some magnificent sauternes and McWilliam's always had a series of whites on the market made from semillon or blends of semillon and pinot or aucerot which were reasonable in price and top quality. This indicates, at least to my satisfaction, that white wines and red wines do not often show the same top quality factors in the same year.

Even through the dry years of the 1960s, top quality

whites kept reappearing, mainly from Lindeman's and Drayton's. Bob Elliott seemed to be a consistent top quality white man. A series of his wines from 1955 to the present day would, I feel sure, show little deviation from year to year. This leads me to believe that the whites of the valley generally show top quality factors more frequently than the reds.

Is it, then the extremely diverse behaviour of weather which is the cause of the great variation of quality in the Hunter? Once again I quote Max Lake: 'Those who deny this vintage variation in the Hunter have not made a sufficiently careful study of the wines – or have an ulterior motive. It will be necessary to follow the fortunes of Hunter vineyards through all the cycles of the weather – drought, fire, hail and flooding – for a long period yet, before any generally predictable pattern emerges, if it ever does.'

On the information I have researched, some of which is summarized above, it seems that, apart from the wine-maker, the most important quality factor in Hunter wines is this weather variation. It does indeed appear that, unless the area experienced quite a deal of bad weather, we might not see quality white wines from here at all.

WYBONG/SANDY HOLLOW
Penfold's set the pattern in 1961 when they spurned the well-established Pokolbin area and planted a new Hunter Valley vineyard 112 km away to the north-west. The shrewd and worldly-wise Ken Commins took his cue from Penfold's and purchased 170 hectares of land suitable for planting vines at Hollydeen 2 km down the Wybong Creek from Penfold's Wybong Park. Well advised by local viticulturalists, Ken Commins hoped to secure all the quality advantages of the Hunter Valley while avoiding the economic hazards of the Pokolbin/Rothbury area.

His vineyard manager, Harry Tulloch, took cuttings from selected clones of 600 cabernet sauvignon vines growing on Max Lake's property and planted them in the rich alluvial soil of the **Hollydene Estate**. (This is the name Ken

Commins chose for his vineyard.) Today these vines are bearing. Hollydene impresses me as a vineyard venture most likely to succeed and most likely to produce very high quality wine both red and white.

The combined brains of several experts in their own fields have given rise to a vineyard and winery complex that is unique in Australia. The financial acumen of Ken Commins has been employed to explore all avenues in the choice of best vineyard land and winery equipment.

Hollydene Estate occupies a situation adjacent to the Creek. I have examined a soil profile cut out by the action of the stream. At least 6 metres of dark red and brown alluvium indicated the underground structure of the nearby fields. The water table in an average year is 9 to 12 metres so wells are employed to supplement rain in dry spells. The richness of the soil is indicated by the luxuriant growth of weeds which must cause near dementia to the vineyard manager.

The winery is constructed in a circle. Huge stainless steel pre-draining and fermenting tanks made by Ron Potter of Griffith surround the stadium of reinforced concrete. As the grapes arrive they are tipped into an Amos roller crusher. From that moment the juice is protected from air by a coating of carbon dioxide gas until the wine is ready for bottling. Juice is extracted from the crushed grapes by a Coq auto-regulated continuous press (naturally coated with CO_2). For white wines the juice is 'centrifuged' before fermentation. This is to remove all solids such as grape pulp which act as catalysts to cause oxidation. Time is an important factor at this stage and in this action. Hollydene endeavours to move the material as little as possible. Hence the winery is in the shape of a wheel with the must, juice and fermented wine moving backwards and forwards along the spokes to settle finally in the central underground polymer lined tanks.

Judging from the wine that has been made from grapes grown at Penfold's Wybong project, by David Hordern at Wybong Estate and by Hollydene, it appears that this area is another classical district comparable in quality to Pokolbin/Rothbury.

All this area is sometimes called the 'Upper Hunter' but for reasons explained elsewhere, this is too wide a term. Hence I have grouped all the sub areas which seem to be closely related by local conditions of climate, soil, elevation above sea level and topography as 'Wybong/Sandy Hollow'. The wineries covered by this title are **Penfold's Dalwood Estate**, **Hollydene**, **Hordern's** and the **Hordern-Smith** venture on Hordern's property, **Chateau Douglas**, **Mt Dangar**, **Peachey**, **Richmond Grove**, **Stair** and **Erinvale**.

HUNTER FLATS

The country adjacent to the Hunter River is sometimes known as 'the Hunter corridor'. In the centre of this corridor there are the flats right next to the river itself and its tributaries. They consist of alluvium and colluvium. Sometimes they are gently undulating. They have much the same climate in the centre of the valley but to the west and north they are adjacent to and run into the hills and plateau country.

Viticulturally, therefore, there is bound to be a difference. Shadows in the morning and afternoon are experienced over the vineyards of the hills of which the flats will not have the benefit.

The wines from the flats are very different from those grown in the Pokolbin/Rothbury and Wybong/Sandy Hollow areas. Vineyards included in these flats are at Branxton, Belford, Fordwich, Glendon Brook, Jerry's Plains and Denman and are: **Ladera** (Carr), **Wyndham Estate**, **Fordwich** (Elliott, Tulloch, Saxonvale), **Belford** (Elliott), **Arrowfield**, **Glendon Brook**, **Horseshoe**, **Mindaribba**.

MUDGEE

Mudgee is 274 km north-west of Sydney in fairly mountainous country. The town itself has two interesting features: first, it was designed by the same man who laid out the city of Melbourne, Robert Hoddle; secondly it was the birthplace of Henry Lawson.

Like so many successful areas in all parts of the world the planting of vines at Mudgee was only a matter of luck.

Today, no-one would invest capital in vineyards unless he spent many hundreds of dollars first, investigating the suitability of the climate, aspect and soil for grape growing. In the early days of Australia there was no time nor indeed sources of knowledge for this kind of thing.

The new settler from Europe, enthusiastic about wine-making, simply selected a plot of ground he thought would grow grapes successfully and either bought it or sought it as a grant from the government.

In some cases his choice turned out to be a remarkable piece of good fortune for the wines he made were good and production was plentiful.

Thus it was at Mudgee. One can imagine settlers coming from the British Isles and Europe, wondering where to go to begin a new life on the land.

Many stories would be coming into Sydney of the fertile lands all around, of the great potential there was in the ranges separating the coastal regions from the great plains on the other side of the mountains.

By 1830, all the arable land along the coast and along the river valleys would have been taken up. Recently arrived migrants would be looking eagerly at the country higher up in the hills where no-one so far had settled.

For most of them it was a matter of getting a plot of cultivable soil anywhere to put into practice the agricultural pursuits with which they were familiar.

So Mudgee was settled. Some of the early settlers were from Germany and planted vines as well as crops. In a country short of alcoholic beverages there was a ready sale for their wines immediately.

Little did these migrants realize that they were beginning a new industry which would bloom into fulfilment a hundred and thirty years later. During these years, depressions, droughts, failure of industries in the areas and a

hundred other factors had resulted in the Mudgee area
being very small as a wine growing centre.

It settled down in the early part of this century to making
and selling fortified wines – like port and muscat. This
was natural since the new nation of Australians had not been
educated to drinking fine table wines. A few wealthy
Englishmen who owned fine homes in Sydney and Melbourne had their private cellars which they filled with
beautiful imported wines and a few local vintages. The
great mass of the people, however, had no knowledge of
wines and had, for the most part, been used to drinking
beer and cheap spirits in their original lands. Fortified
wines at a low price were thus to be preferred to the expensive spirits available in Australia. It was not worth Mudgee
winemakers producing more than a minimal quantity of
table wines.

This condition remained until the late 1960s. By this
time, Australians had begun to learn and appreciate the
value of unfortified wine.

Suddenly Sydney folk began to ask the Mudgee wine-
makers for table wines as well as for port, sherry and muscat.
Unfortunately, only one of the winemakers remained.
He was Jack Roth who owned **Craigmoor Winery** and
Eurunderee Vineyard.

Van Heyst and Co. Ltd, a finance company headed by
Cyrille Van Heyst, had become interested in the area as a
potential unfortified wine producing region and purchased
the entire property. They installed Pieter Van Gent, who
had been winemaker with Penfolds at Minchinbury for
ten years, as manager and winemaker at Craigmoor.

Pieter almost worked miracles. He converted the decrepit
winery into a clean working unit. He revived the old
vineyards and planted new vines on newly acquired land.
He began to make first quality wine. Very quickly people
began to realize what had taken place. Craigmoor and
Mudgee had begun to scintillate like a new constellation
in the world of Australian wine.

Mudgee is situated near the Hunter Valley. The difference

between the two districts is altitude. Mudgee vineyards are about 488 metres above sea level. This makes it a much cooler place than the Hunter which is in many parts not much higher than sea level.

I have tasted many of the wines coming from here in the last two or three years and I am tremendously impressed with them. With so much rain and cloud in northern N.S.W. this summer it would not have been surprising to see a light vintage from Mudgee; but being over the range from the Hunter and being higher has in fact meant that Mudgee escaped much of the bad weather.

In consequence the dry reds, made from shiraz and cabernet sauvignon, had a very good deep and, in the case of cabernet, very dense colour with full flavour and abundant fruit quality.

The chardonnay was soft with good acid and beautifully balanced and the semillon was clean, very fruity with nice acid. As these two wines are put together by Craigmoor and are marketed as **Semillon Chardonnay** we can look forward to the 1974 vintage. The 1973 bottlings of this wine and its companion, **Trebbiano**, are of very high quality and should be able to be purchased without much trouble.

Craigmoor Wines have planted shiraz, cabernet, chardonnay, traminer and sauvignon blanc. The straight chardonnay and the chardonnay-semillon blend are magnificent white wines which have picked up quite a number of show medals.

Although Craigmoor's Eurunderee vineyard is the oldest in the area, new ones which are producing extremely good wines are **Augustine**, **Mudgee Wines** and **Huntingdon Estate**.

Mudgee's claim to recognition as a very great vineyard area is largely based on the fact that it has similar climatic conditions to the Hunter Valley.

Mr Richard Smart of the N.S.W. Department of Agriculture in an, as yet, unpublished paper on the four areas of Cessnock, Mudgee, M.I.A. and Richmond (Rooty Hill) makes the statement 'it does appear that Mudgee has the most suitable climate for quality dry table wines production, and one would expect table wines from this area to be superior to those of the Hunter River area.'

An examination of comparative day degrees, altitude, cloud cover, sunlight hours and rainfall would seem to support that claim.

Nonetheless, I feel that we have not seen a sufficient number of outstanding wines from Mudgee to classify the area as 'outstanding'. It has not had a long enough history of producing great wines. It stands in a similar way to Keppoch in South Australia, where we are tempted to argue that because Keppoch is so close to Coonawarra that it, too, should be classified as 'outstanding'.

I cannot see that it follows. We shall have to wait and see.

Meanwhile I am quite sure that the classification of Mudgee as a 'very great area' is warranted by all the data available.

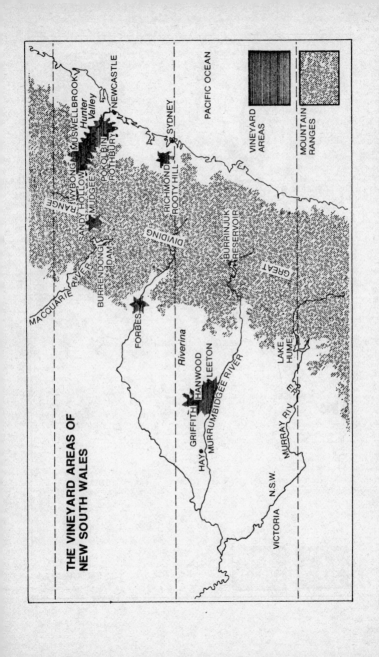

THE VINEYARD AREAS OF
NEW SOUTH WALES

PACIFIC OCEAN

VINEYARD AREAS

MOUNTAIN RANGES

Newcastle
Muswellbrook
Hunter Valley
Kwybong
Pokolbin
Rothbury
SYDNEY
Sandy Hollow
Mudgee
Richmond
Rooty Hill
Burrendong Dam
Burrinjuk Reservoir
GREAT
MACQUARIE RIVER
DIVIDING RANGE
Forbes
Riverina
Griffith
Hanwood
Leeton
Murrumbidgee River
Lake Hume
Hay
Murray River
N.S.W.
VICTORIA

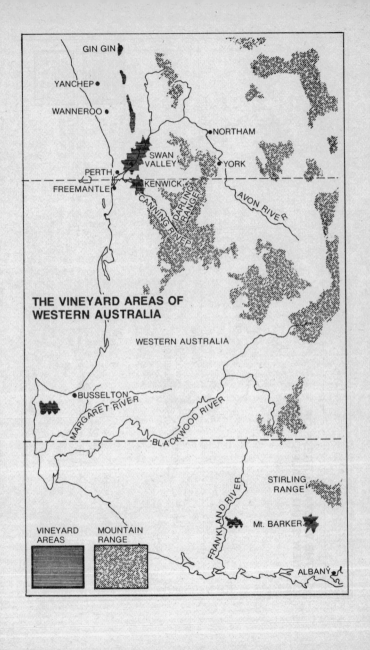

THE VINEYARD AREAS OF WESTERN AUSTRALIA

GIN GIN

YANCHEP

WANNEROO

NORTHAM

SWAN VALLEY

PERTH

YORK

FREEMANTLE

KENWICK

DARLING RANGE

CANNING RIVER

AVON RIVER

WESTERN AUSTRALIA

BUSSELTON

MARGARET RIVER

BLACKWOOD RIVER

STIRLING RANGE

FRANKLAND RIVER

Mt. BARKER

ALBANY

VINEYARD AREAS

MOUNTAIN RANGE

8 Western Australia, Queensland, Tasmania, other regions and new areas

Western Australia

In Chapter 3 I make the statement that the Swan Valley of Western Australia must be considered one of the flagon wine regions of Australia, and I now support my case with several arguments.

I am quite aware that some wines from the Swan Valley, specifically **Houghton's White Burgundy** and **Sandalford** whites of recent years, have been magnificent. That fact does not change the conclusion I have come to, that 'What makes an area outstanding is its flow of top quality wines from the whole area in a majority of years'.

Delighted as I have been sometimes with Swan Valley whites, I have seen too many wines both red and white and from all makers of this area which portrayed very clearly the climatic conditions of the area.

These climatic conditions are such that the Swan Valley is not likely to be classified as anything but a 'very good' wine region. The summer temperatures are too high, the heat summation is too great and the sunlight hours too many.

New areas are being opened up around Margaret River and Mount Barker. Because of climatic conditions here I have classified them under 'very great wines' with an asterisk: *Vineyards which have not produced sufficient wines for quality to be assessed but which are in locations which indicate great quality.

New Areas

So great has been the development of new vineyards in Victoria, New South Wales and South Australia in the last ten years that the expansion taking place in Western Australia has hardly been noticed.

Yet new plantings in the Swan Valley have been considerable and at Gin-Gin, about eighty kilometres north of Perth, Valencia have begun a project, which is now producing effectively, of over eighty hectares.

The most interesting new vineyards, though, are in the south-west. In 1963 the Western Australian Department of Agriculture planted an experimental vineyard of two hectares on the property of Tony and Betty Pearse near Mt Barker.

This region is mostly heavily timbered country with rolling hills and ranges of low mountains thrusting down to the sea. The many acres that have been cleared are proving highly successful for grazing and crops.

A glance at the map of the south-west shows why it escapes the drying east winds that are the chief scourge of the Swan Valley. Oceans to the east and the west of this corner of the continent encase it in cool breezes during the summer months. Snow falls on the Porangurup and Stirling Ranges.

The Department of Agriculture leased the new vineyard from the Pearses for ten years on the understanding that the Pearses looked after the vineyard under departmental guidance and that the vineyard should be theirs after ten years.

Tony does the heavy work such as driving the tractor and Betty, who is an ebullient housewife in her early thirties, does the pruning, training and tying of the vines and organizes the picking of the grapes.

This couple have plenty to do as well as caring for a small vineyard. They have 300 hectares of grazing land to tend and the breeding of lambs from carefully chosen stock keeps them busy fifteen hours a day.

Yet I have rarely seen such enthusiasm for grapes even among old timers in the east. They intend to build their own winery.

I tasted the 1974 Rhine Riesling. It really is a beautiful

wine. The cabernet sauvignon had a dense purple colour and an extremely strong bouquet with a pleasant aroma something like that of stewed plums. The wine was very full on the first and middle palates, pleasantly astringent and it left a very pleasant clean flavour on the tongue.

These wines were made at Sandalford Winery. Naturally, there are not enough available yet for sale. Earlier vintages have been exhibited in shows and won several awards.

Dr Cullity, a leading heart specialist in Perth, three years ago began an experimental vineyard just north of Margaret River in the Busselton area. He was quickly followed by Dr Pannell, a local medical practitioner. The Roe family, who own Sandalford last year purchased 340 hectares near the Cullity vineyard and have forty hectares planted with cabernet sauvignon, rhine riesling and verdelho. They intend eventually to have 121 hectares under vine.

Whether this southern area will produce wine of the quality of other cool climate areas such as Coonawarra, Clare and Great Western has to be seen. Scientific data seems to indicate that it will but scientific data can be used to satisfy almost everybody. There is no area in the world that is exactly similar to another.

One thing is certain. If Western Australia is to make wines which compare with the bordeaux and burgundies of France, this is where they will be made.

Queensland

There are considerable hectares of vineyards at Roma and in the hilly areas of the Great Divide near the N.S.W. border. Roma has not suitable climatic conditions for the production of table wines and no table wines are made here.

The small vineyards of the Southern highlands may perhaps produce table wines worthy of consideration, but at this stage the winemakers have not shown sufficient wines or, for that matter sufficient interest, to warrant their being classified.

That does not eliminate them from classification for all time. In future years it may be shown that they do indeed produce wines which are at least able to be classified as 'very good'.

Tasmania

It appears that vines are likely to grow well in both the Tamar and Derwent valleys. The difficulty will be in choosing the correct varieties so that the grapes will ripen every year. I have no doubt that, if vineyards can be successfully developed, very great wines will be made. All the climatic conditions necessary for the production of high quality wines are present, except perhaps sufficient sun heat. Vineyards in both the Tamar and Derwent valleys produced wine in 1974.

Other Regions

The **Richmond** area just out of Sydney, and Rooty Hill in particular, seem to have all the conditions necessary for the production of top quality table wines. The reputation of **Penfold's Trameah** goes right back to the twenties. There is no doubt that it was one of the greatest white wines Australia has produced, and it is more than likely that the quality of the earlier whites could be recaptured in wines made there today.

I reiterate, however, that no area can be graded as a quality area, unless it produces a continuous flow of high quality wines which are commercially available – even if only in small quantities.

This does not seem to be the case with Rooty Hill. It appears that Penfold's are prepared to release only wines from here that are blended with wines from other areas.

It is more than likely, in addition, that the future of grape growing at Richmond could be in doubt. With residential and industrial development taking place at such a great rate in the area it is probable that vineyards will be as out of place, as they are at Magill in Adelaide. There is no point in classifying vineyards which exist under this condition.

Forbes in N.S.W. is a very small area and fortified wines seem to be the main output. Climatic conditions would place it very much in line with the Murrumbidgee Irrigation Area. Thus it does not appear in my classification of vineyards.

MARGARET RIVER AND MT BARKER IN WESTERN AUSTRALIA

Obviously all hopes for these areas are based on climatic data. That gathered by the Department of Agriculture in this state gives every indication that a high quality area is being developed, but there are so many factors in the production of quality wine that all we can say is, 'let us hope'.

Areas covered by the Vintage Chart

If I made a vintage chart covering each individual area in Australia, it would be too unwieldy. In any case it is not necessary.

Weather is the reason why one year is better or worse than another. In any wine region the weather is much the same. I have grouped, therefore, areas which are subject to identical weather patterns.

They are:

1. *Clare/Watervale* – or that part of the Mt Lofty Range roughly between the towns of Watervale and Clare and including all the vineyards surrounding these towns.
2. *The Barossa* – including the Barossa Valley itself and the nearby Barossa Ranges, the low ranges of hills down as far as Adelaide and the vineyards on the outskirts of Adelaide.
3. *Southern Vales* – including Reynella, Coromandel Valley, Happy Valley, the hills around Clarendon, McLaren Vale and Langhorne Creek.
4. *South-east South Australia* – including Coonawarra and Keppoch.
5. *South-west Victoria* – including Drumborg, Great Western, Ararat and Avoca.

6. *North-east Victoria* – including Rutherglen, Corowa, Milawa and Taminick.
7. *Goulburn Valley* – including all areas north of Chateau Tahbilk and Mitchelton.
8. *Hunter Valley* – including the area of Mudgee which is in the ranges just out of the Valley.

I have not included any vineyard area which has not been classified as Outstanding, Very Great or Great since the slight variation of quality in other areas does not justify the compilation of a vintage chart.

WINEMAKERS ARE NOT THE ONES TO ASSESS THE QUALITY OF A VINTAGE YEAR

I am aware that winemakers themselves will apply different criteria for a vintage year to mine.

I am sure that in France in 1959 it was the winemakers and wine merchants who set the whole world agog with their claim that it was the greatest vintage ever. They were carried away with the perfect conditions for vintage of that summer – very hot weather, no rain, no pests, perfect growth of the vines, beautiful development of the berries.

It did not take very long for the connoisseurs to sort out the facts. Hence today 1959 rates only 6 out of 7 in the red wine districts of France and is overshadowed by 1961.

In Australia winemakers are apt to become critical of a year because of rain or poor cropping or disease. These factors do not necessarily mean a poor year for quality and the true assessment cannot be made until two or three years later.

THE VINTAGE CHART ASSESSES ONLY DRY RED WINES AND DRY WHITE WINES

High quality Dry Red Wine Areas and Dry White Wine Areas are well defined and are set out clearly in this book.

We do not have any such clearly defined areas for an unfortified sweet wine such as sauternes or spaetlese riesling. Except at Drumborg, we have had no *noble rot* caused by the mould *botrytis cinerea* in our white grapes.

The consequence is that they never become sweet enough to make naturally sweet wines. Our sweet white wines are made either by adding grape sugar or stopping fermentation artificially so as to retain some sweetness of the grape. Since the grape must has not enough sugar to allow this to happen without alcoholic content suffering, we finish up with an inferior wine.

Rosé has not won much acclaim in Australia. Who can say where our best rosé wines come from? Very often they come from irrigation areas. Sometimes they are blends.

WINE SHOWS ARE LITTLE INDICATION OF THE COMPARATIVE VALUE OF VARIOUS VINTAGES

Awards are handed out at Wine Shows for wines of current vintage, of previous vintage or 'open' class, that is of any vintage.

This means that gold medals are given to the best wines of any particular class of one vintage except in open class. In open class gold medals are given to the best wines of the class irrespective of how old they are.

The judges, therefore, are not concerned about relating one vintage to another. Wines of a very poor vintage year will receive a proportion of gold, silver and bronze medals just as wines of an exceptional vintage year.

Gold medals, therefore, are no indication of the excellence or otherwise of any vintage year.

Conclusion

Quality, it seems to me, in dry red and dry white table wines is a matter of sugar development in the grape for any one particular year.

It seems that the two extremes in quality areas are positions where grapes do not ripen and positions where the sugar rises so quickly that it is present in sufficient quantities while the sun's rays are still hot enough to cook it.

Thus any particular spot where this 'cooking of sugar' does not occur is likely to produce high quality table wines.

It may be so far north or south that ripening takes all the summer and by the time sufficient sugar has built up the atmosphere is quite cool.

It may be in a steep river valley where the sun shines on the vines only half a day every day. It could be on the side of a hill which gets only the morning or afternoon sun, or where it gets the shade of a hill for a great part of a summer's day. It could be an area where there is a great deal of summer cloud and the burning rays of the hot summer sun do not reach the vines.

Perhaps it is in a latitude where the sun's rays are direct and where the clouds are few but its height above sea level means a lesser temperature than similar areas lower down. Perhaps it is close to the sea and in this particular spot a cool wind blows from the ocean every summer afternoon.

Anything that will prevent this cooking is good. Hot low flat inland areas are never likely to make high quality table wines. Southerly vineyards, high altitude vineyards, hill sheltered vineyards are.

The comparison of the area day degrees and sunlight hours are only a most general guide. In point of fact they are useless when related to a particular vineyard unless the figures relating to that particular vineyard can be obtained.

In an area where the meteorologist has recorded day degrees of 4000 in a six months growing period, several vineyards in favourable positions could be exposed to only half that amount of heat. The comparison of sunlight hours is full of pitfalls for the unwary. In December the number of hours of sunlight at Drumborg 38° south is many more than at Cessnock 33° south, simply because the closer an area is to the equator in summer the shorter the day. However that does not mean Drumborg is hotter than Cessnock. Obviously it is not. The development of sugar is, therefore, slower and the 'cooking' of sugar does not occur.

On the other hand, if a vineyard at Cessnock is not exposed to the direct rays of the summer sun for more than half a day, it is just as well off as a vineyard at Drumborg which is.

In any vintage, to a certain degree, the higher the latitude at which a vineyard is situated, the hotter the summer is, the better it is for quality wine in that vintage; the lower the latitude, the cooler the summer it is, the better it is for quality wine that vintage.

Once again this statement must be qualified by reference to the aspect of the vineyard. In the Rhine Valley, for example, it is usual for the quality of wines to be related to the heat of the summer; but at Rudesheim where the vines are on a steep slope facing north a very hot summer means that the sun burns the grapes and the wines are lacking in finesse.

On the other hand, in the Hunter Valley, vineyards well protected from the direct rays of the sun would suffer from a cool wet summer. They would not receive enough heat and the pigments in red grapes would not develop sufficiently. Hence the red wines would be lacking in colour and body.

Perhaps it is mystifying that even in a cold wet summer the sugar builds up in the grapes at Cessnock sufficiently to harvest in the middle of February, whereas at Drumborg harvesting can never take place before April.

Here again it is only a matter of heat. It is much hotter from 6 a.m. to 6 p.m. at Cessnock in January than it is at Drumborg from 5 a.m. to 7 p.m. in any year dry or wet. Hence sugar builds up in January at Cessnock but not at Drumborg.

The computations are innumerable. In the long run, what matters is experience. At this stage, we know whence come our top quality wines. We can spend the next hundred years trying to analyze the precise conditions which make for this top quality.

INDEX

INDEX OF WINES

Durif dry red shiraz 33

Mudgee Wines: cabernet sauvignon 34; hermitage 34

Norman: Angle Vale burgundy 36; Angle Vale claret 27

Olive Farm: burgundy 35; claret 35

Orlando: Barossa cabernet 26; Barossa hermitage 26; cabernet 73; hermitage 73; hermitage cabernet 31; Miramba vintage 31

O'Shea, Maurice: cabernet sauvignon 1944 169; cabernet sauvignon 1948 169

O'Shea, Stephen: hermitage 1952 182

Parri: burgundy 35; cabernet 35; claret 35

Penfold's: bin 2 shiraz Mataro 23, 61; bin 28 Kalimna shiraz 23, 61; bin 128 Coonawarra claret 22, 61; special bin 333 30; bin 389 cabernet shiraz 23, 53, 61, 119–120; bin 426 shiraz oelliade 23; bin 707 Kalimna cabernet sauvignon 23, 61, 119; bin 747 shiraz 23; clarets 610 57; clarets 707 51; Coonawarra claret 73; Dalwood burgundy 36; Dalwood claret 36; Dalwood Hermitage 36; Grange hermitage 22, 53, 59–61, 73, 108–9, 114, 145; St Henri claret 22; Wybong Park cabernet sauvignon 26; Wybong Park hermitage 26; Wybong Park other grape varieties 26

Peters: claret 35; shiraz 35

Pokolbin Winemakers: hermitage 30

Pott's: Constantia 142; malbec dry red 142

Quelltaler: San Carlo claret 36

Renmano: Montessa claret cabernet malbec 33

Redman (O & L): Redman claret 22, 73; Coonawarra claret 109

Riverside: burgundy 35; claret 35; hermitage 35

Romalo: champagne 71

Rossetto: Beelgara cabernet sauvignon 34; Beelgara dry red 34

Rothbury Estate: Rothbury Estate label 38

Rovalley: cabernet shiraz 31; shiraz claret 31

Ryecroft: cabernet sauvignon 28; shiraz 32

Sandalford: cabernet sauvignon 35; shiraz 35; Pearse cabernet sauvignon 195

Saltram: selected vintage burgundy 36; selected vintage claret 27; Mamre Brook cabernet 24

Seaview: cabernet sauvignon 24; cabernet shiraz 24; cabernet 73, 136

Seppelt's: bin 113/68 Gr Western hermitage 1968 165; Chalambar burgundy 36, 156, 158, 163; EC4 hermitage cabernet 27; Gt Western reds 73; hermitage 1968/GW176 Keppoch 25; Keppoch 25; Moyston claret 36, 156, 158, 163; sparkling burgundy 156, 163; The Hermitage 151

Seven Hill: dry red table wine 31

South Coast Winery: McLaren Park shiraz 32

Southern Vales Co-op.: special bin cabernet 28; special bin hermitage 28

St Hallet's: Carl special dry red claret 31

St Clare: cabernet sauvignon 23; cabernet malbec shiraz 23; cabernet shiraz 23; malbec shiraz 23

Stanley Wine Co.: Clare special